Collins
revision guides

Do**Brilliantly**

A2 Business Studies

Exam practice at its **best**

- **Stuart Merrills**
- **Series Editor: Jayne de Courcy**

Contents

Published by HarperCollins*Publishers* Ltd
77–85 Fulham Palace Road
London W6 8JB

www.**Collins**Education.com
On-line support for schools and colleges

First published 2003
10 9 8 7 6 5 4 3
ISBN 0 00 714877 1

British Library Cataloguing in Publication Data
A catalogue record for this book is available from the British Library.

Edited by Margaret Shepherd
Production by Jack Murphy
Book design by Bob Vickers
Printed and bound in China by Imago

Acknowledgements
With grateful thanks to Dawn for her patience and understanding during this project.

The Author and Publishers are grateful to the following for permission to reproduce copyright material:
AQA: pp. 37, 38, 39, 40, 41, 50, 51, 52, 64, 88, 89, 90.
AQA examination questions are reproduced by permission of the Assessment and Qualifications Alliance.

Every effort has been made to contact the holders of copyright material, but if any have been inadvertently overlooked, the Publishers will be pleased to make the necessary arrangements at the first opportunity.

You might also like to visit:
www.**fire**and**water**.com
The book lover's website

How this book will help you
by Stuart Merrills

Exam practice – how to answer questions better

This book will help you to improve your performance in your A2 Business Studies exams.

I have marked many exam papers where students haven't used the knowledge that they have as effectively as they could. This means that they don't get the grade they are capable of achieving.

To get a good grade in A2 Business Studies you need a good understanding of the subject matter, an up-to-date awareness of current business issues, good communication skills and **good exam technique**. Your textbook and teacher will help you develop your knowledge and understanding. **This book will help you improve your exam technique, so that you can make the most effective use of what you know.**

Each chapter in this book is broken down into four separate parts, aimed at giving you the chance to practice and develop your exam technique. It may also help improve your knowledge as well.

❶ Exam Question, Student's Answer and 'How to score full marks'

Each chapter starts with an exam question of the sort you will find on a real A2 Business Studies paper, followed by a typical student's answer.

The 'How to score full marks' sections, then critically examine these answers and show you where and how the answers could be improved, e.g. by explaining what the question is asking for, pointing out missing knowledge or discussing technique and approach to developing a good response. **This means that when you meet these types of questions in your exams, you will know how to tackle them successfully.**

At A2, the questions require a developed response, so I have provided information on alternative approaches, highlighting useful lines of argument and concentrating on the skills of analysis and evaluation so you can see what examiners such as myself are looking for.

❷ 'Don't forget . . .' boxes

These boxes highlight some of the more **common mistakes that I see every year in students' exam papers.** These include both errors in knowledge and understanding (such as the application of particular theories) as well as mistakes in exam technique.

These boxes are designed as a quick reference guide to building your exam technique.

❸ 'Key points to remember'

These are the **most important aspects that you need to cover when revising the topic.** They give you an overview of each topic area so that you can spot any gaps or weaknesses in your knowledge.

Remember that a book of this size cannot be a comprehensive revision guide – that's what your class notes and textbook are for!

❹ Question to try, Answers and Examiner's hints and comments

Chapters 2, 3, 4 and 6 end with a **question for you to try answering**. Don't cheat! Sit down and try to answer as if you were in an exam. Time yourself – this will help make the practice real. Try to remember all that you've read earlier and put it into practice. I have given some **'Examiner's hints'** to help you tackle the more difficult aspects of the question.

When you've written your answer, check it through and then turn to the back of the book. There you'll find an answer to the question you've just done. These answers are of a good 'A' grade standard. I have added my **'Examiner's comments'** to show you exactly why it is such a good answer.

Compare your answer with the answer given. If you feel yours wasn't as good, note down the areas in which you feel the model answer given was better and re-write your answer to develop your technique and improve your grade.

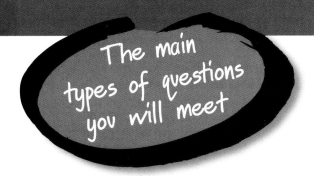
The main types of questions you will meet

The most popular exam board for A2 Business Studies is AQA. The questions in this book are written mainly for the AQA style questions. However, the approach used by OCR and Edexcel is similar and the information on exam technique, the 'Don't forget' boxes and the 'Key points' sections are all useful whichever board you are with.

Case studies

The format of these is a detailed and in-depth scenario. These questions are used to test the higher order skills, i.e. they focus on assessing your ability to **analyse and evaluate situations**. Papers 4 and 6 for AQA and all OCR papers consist of case studies. For these papers, it is especially important that you are able to interpret and understand the **command words** such as **'discuss'** or **'evaluate'**. These are explained in more depth on page 5.

Case studies will often require you to offer solutions to business problems or analyse situations and propose business actions. Frequently, case studies are used to integrate the assessment of various topics. For example, the AQA paper 4 case study examines the topics of marketing, accounting and finance, people and operations management at the same time. You would be expected to answer two questions on each area.

In order to achieve a good grade in response to questions assessed via a case study, **it is vital that you relate your answers to the scenario and the situation given to you**. This means you need to be able to place your answers in a **realistic context** and focus on how the firm in the case is likely and **able** to react.

Business reports

For AQA unit 5W taken by those candidates not following the coursework option, you will be required to write a business report worth 40 marks. This exam takes the format of presenting you with a brief company outline and a series of appendices containing a range of data varying from financial information to economic indicators and/or market analysis and production figures.

The focus of this is for you to take the role of a business consultant, financial advisor or manager and write a report commenting on the pros and cons of a particular decision. This exam requires you to demonstrate **knowledge, analysis and evaluation** in the interpretation of the data and in reaching a conclusion or recommendation for the company in the scenario.

This exam is covered in more detail in Chapter 3.

Essays

This form of question is used mainly to assess the skill of **evaluation** and is also part of AQA unit 5W. Each essay is worth 40 marks and you have a choice of one essay from four.

Essays ask you to examine a topic from more than one perspective and consider a range of arguments. Essays require you to write at length about a given topic and think about all the possible issues and aspects that it raises. **Your aim is to discuss a range of implications and consider the validity of each argument and, through a logical sequence, reach a conclusion.** Often in Business Studies the answer will be 'it depends' and so you are required to demonstrate **'evaluation'** by determining which factors are the most significant or most likely.

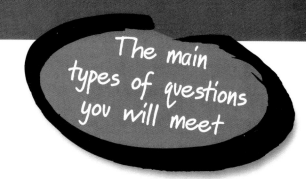
The main types of questions you will meet

Command words

Look carefully at the command word given in the question **and the mark allocation of the question**. This will help you formulate the type of answer needed **and the amount of time you should allocate for your response**. Very common mistakes in exam technique are that students either fail to develop arguments sufficiently or overdevelop answers to questions that require simple responses so they run out of time on the final questions.

Explanatory questions

These are usually identified by the command words or phrases:
- 'Explain', 'Outline', 'Distinguish between . . .' or they may require calculations.

These require you **to offer relevant subject knowledge and an explanation of how it might apply to the scenario given**. You need to expand upon a relevant point or influential factor to demonstrate your understanding of the term or theory presented.

This type of question will only be found on paper 4 for AQA candidates.

Analytical questions

These can be distinguished by the words or phrases:
- 'Examine', 'Explain why', 'Analyse' or 'Consider'.

These need to be answered in more depth. They often require advantages and/or disadvantages of business actions or situations to be discussed. **You need to demonstrate knowledge, apply it to the scenario or situation given and then consider further implications, knock-on effects or cause-and-effect relationships**. You need to explain in detail the process whereby cause brings about the end result. To answer these questions well you need to use a continuous prose style of writing in well-structured and developed paragraphs. Remember, in Business Studies there are two sides to every situation.

Again these questions will only appear on AQA paper 4.

Evaluative questions

These can be recognised by the words or phrases:
- 'Evaluate', 'Discuss', 'To what extent' or 'Recommend'.

This type of question requires you to reach a judgement. This may be weighing up the relative strengths (pros and cons) of your arguments in order to reach a conclusion. Equally, it may be discussing the likelihood of factors occurring so that you develop a judgement of which factors should be considered the most important. Again, you must put your answers in the context of the scenario presented.

Some questions on AQA paper 4 and **all questions on AQA papers 5 and 6 require you to demonstrate evaluation**.

Level-of-response marking

All Business Studies papers are marked using level-of-response marking. This uses a number of descriptors against which your work is assessed. The table below shows the level-of-response marking grid for an **evaluative question** worth 14 marks.

	Content 3 marks	Application* 2 marks	Analysis 3 marks	Evaluation 6 marks
Level 3				**5–6 marks** Mature, reasoned judgement in argument and/or conclusions
Level 2	**3 marks** Clear and valid understanding shown	**2 marks** Sound application of issues to the case	**3 marks** Good analysis of issues to the case	**3–4 marks** Good judgement in argument and/or conclusions
Level 1	**1–2 marks** Some understanding shown	**1 mark** Some application of issues to the case	**1–2 marks** Limited analysis of issues	**1–2 marks** Limited judgement shown
Level 0	**0 marks** No understanding shown	**0 marks** No application of issues to the case	**0 marks** No analysis offered	**0 marks** No judgement shown

*Application marks are available for specifically putting your answer in context to the scenario.

- **To attain full marks for this sort of question you must demonstrate all the different skills shown** – content, application, analysis and evaluation – and move through the levels of each skill. For example, a student who just provided a bullet point list for his answer would only be showing **limited content,** and thus receive 1 or 2 marks.

- **A single paragraph of continuous prose that develops an argument relevant to the scenario** might well gain content level one (1 mark), level two application (2 marks) and limited or sound analysis (1 or 2 marks). Total marks: 4 or 5.

- **An answer that offers good analysis of several points relating directly to the scenario, in a number of separate paragraphs weighing each considered point, and drawing to a logical conclusion or reasoned judgement,** would receive top of level two marks for content, application and analysis and top of level three for evaluation and hence a maximum of 14 marks.

- **Important note:** You can reach the top of each level independently, e.g. it is possible to get level 2 content, application and analysis but include no evaluation in your answer thus scoring: Content 3 marks, Application 2 marks, Analysis 3 marks and Evaluation 0 marks. Total marks: 8.

- **A key point at A2 is to note the weight of marks given to the skill of evaluation.** The marking grid above is typical of AQA A2 assessment on Papers 4 and 6.

- **It is, therefore, very important that you understand the key command words so that you know what skills you have to demonstrate in your answers**. The questions in this book will give you excellent practice in developing the necessary skills to move through the levels of each assessment objective.

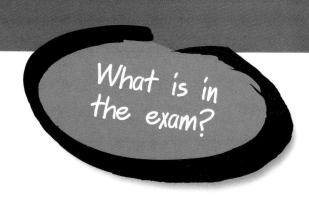
What is in the exam?

For the AQA Business Studies exam, you have to sit three papers:	
Paper 4: Business decision making (1 hour 30 minutes)	Unseen case study 15% of A2 award
Paper 5: Business report and essays (1 hour 30 minutes) or coursework option	15% of A2 award
Paper 6: External influences and objectives and strategy (1 hour 30 minutes)	Unseen case study *Synoptic assessment unit 20% of A2 award*

For the OCR Business Studies exam, you have to sit three papers:	
Paper 4: (option choice) (1 hour 30 minutes) Either: Further marketing, or Further accounting, or Further people in organisations, or Further operations management.	All exams are based on unseen case study material 15% of A2 award
Paper 5: Thematic enquiry (1 hour 30 minutes) or coursework option	Report on unseen case study 15% of A2 award
Paper 6: Business strategy (1 hour 30 minutes)	Pre-issued case study *Synoptic assessment unit 20% of A2 award*

For the Edexcel Business Studies exam, you have to sit three papers:	
Unit 4: Analysis and decision making (1 hour 15 minutes)	Compulsory structured questions 15% of A2 award
Unit 5: Business planning (1 hour 30 minutes) or coursework option	Unseen case study 15% of A2 award
Unit 6: Corporate strategy (1 hour 30 minutes)	Pre-released case study *Synoptic assessment unit 20% of A2 award*

Quality of language

All exam papers now carry marks for the assessment of candidates' quality of language. These are additional to the marks allocated to questions. Up to four marks are awarded based on your ability to:

- select and use a form and style of writing appropriate to the subject
- organise relevant information clearly and coherently, using suitable vocabulary and terminology
- present legible text and use accurate spelling, grammar and punctuation.

Structure of this book

Due to the differing pathways offered by the exam boards, this book has been structured in the following way to enable you to gain the best practise whichever specification you follow:

Chapter		Question type
1	Marketing and Finance and Accounting	Case study material
2	People and Operations Management	Case study material
3	The Report Question	Company outline and data for report writing
4	Essay Questions	Essay questions
5	External Influences	Case study material
6	Objectives and Strategy and Synoptic Assessment	Synoptic case study material

Note for AQA candidates

For the paper 4 exam, marketing, finance and accounting, people and operations management are examined together through one case study. To make revision easier, these are split into two areas in Chapters 1 and 2. The 'question to try' for these four areas is a given as a full case study at the end of Chapter 2.

Similarly, paper 6 examines the topics of external influences and objectives and strategy together. In this book, these have been split into Chapters 5 and 6 with a combined assessment question in the final 'question to try' in Chapter 6.

Synoptic assessment

Synoptic assessment is an important part of all A2 exams. Synoptic assessment tests your knowledge and understanding of the subject as a whole, including **how the different aspects that you have studied at AS and A2 are related**. For this reason the exam paper containing the synoptic assessment can only be taken at the end of the course.

Paper 6 is the synoptic assessment paper for all exam boards. This is the most important paper of them all as it carries 20% of your final A2 grade. The emphasis is on strategic understanding and your ability to draw evidence together from any area of the specification. Assessment focuses on the breadth, depth and quality of your analysis and evaluation.

The key to success on these questions is to **think in an integrated manner and take a broad perspective, considering a business and its environment as a whole, not its individual component parts**.

Synopticity and the structuring of answers are covered in depth in Chapter 6.

Exam tips

Before the exam

- Plan your time – use a revision timetable.

- Make sure your notes are organised into topics and exams and that you have covered the entire specification.

- Practice past papers as much as possible – this will help your exam technique and subject knowledge.

- Analyse past papers for topics that have not been examined for a while – use these as a focus point to start your revision.

- Revise your weakest areas of each topic first – then you've got plenty of time to cover them.

During the exam

- **Read the paper carefully** and absorb the material. Remember to use the case studies to help you – if you don't use them when the question tells you to, you will be throwing marks away. A good idea is to **underline key points**.

- **Make a brief plan before writing**. This helps you stay focused on the question and prevents you forgetting key points as you develop your response.

- **Allocate time sensibly**. Use the marks available and the command words as a guide as to how much to write and at what level.

- A simple point but, **read the questions**. If the question says 'advantages' just consider the advantages and vice versa. If it says give two reasons, then give two. Make sure you're doing what the question asks, not what you think it asks.

- **Use paragraphs** to show the examiner when you are starting a new point or demonstrating a new skill.

- Always fully **show your working** for numerical questions. Then, even if you've got it wrong, you can receive some marks for method.

- **Play the game**. Understand what the examiners are looking for and provide it. Use proper terminology and avoid slang and jargon. Stay focused and don't use sweeping statements such as 'all business will'. There are usually two sides to any business action and things 'may' or 'might' happen.

Pet Offensive

In 1974 Holland's was a high street name in the FMCG (Fast Moving Consumer Goods) household market and their products were found on the shelves of most of the large supermarket chains as well as being stocked in regional and local homeware and hardware shops.

Established in 1966 by Craig Holland and his brother Henry in the Attercliffe area of Sheffield, Holland's started by supplying shoe polishes and a limited range of scented blocks of beeswax for polishing furniture. Over the following decade Holland's expanded both the company and the product range, eventually dropping their traditional lines to concentrate on a major factory upgrade to allow the in-house production of aerosol dispensers. They became one of the leading brand names in the air freshener and furniture polish markets. The requirement of a further capital injection in 1975 led to Holland's becoming a private limited company when the brothers asked a selected group of friends and family to become shareholders. Although this led to some loss of control for the brothers, they continued to hold 58% of the shares distributed equally between them. The increase in capital allowed them to purchase their factory and surrounding land and also to embark on a programme of expansion to their existing works.

Throughout the nineties, though, Holland's suffered from a series of setbacks. First, came the introduction of new laws regarding CFC-producing products, which meant that all of Holland's range of goods had to be re-engineered and re-designed to reduce their pollutant effects. Holland's managed to do this but at the expense of most of the reserves the company had built up. Second, came the establishment of the European free market and the increased competition from overseas. This caused Holland's to lose one supermarket supply contract in total and to increase marketing expenditure, at the expense of lower margins, in order to maintain their position in the others. Finally, toward the end of the twentieth century came a lot of product innovation from competitors in the air freshener market, particularly the development of plug-ins and more discreetly designed products.

Now in their sixties, Craig and Henry are determined that the Holland name will survive as a business for their children and grandchildren but they are aware that Holland's is struggling. Three-year sales forecasts indicate a drop in volume (see Appendix A) and value for Holland's products, primarily due to competition from large multinational organisations. Holland's is faced with the risky propositions of product development or of diversification. So they have been conducting research and development into possible new products and markets, with the proviso that any new ventures should make the most of their existing experience, manufacturing capabilities and distribution networks.

Holland's have tried implementing extension strategies in the past but are aware that these may only be short-term solutions. They are ultimately searching for a longer-term resolution to their problems.

The current proposal on the table is for a product called 'Pet Offensive'. This is designed as an odourless (to humans) aerosol spray that acts as a deterrent to cats and dogs. Simply spray the product onto furniture or items such as shoes, and the offensive smell (to animals) will prevent the pet from venturing near the treated article. Thus, pet owners would be able to enjoy their animals whilst also being able to protect valuable items.

The idea appears at first to be a viable one. It fits Holland's criteria for using their existing manufacturing facilities as well as their current contacts and networks. In addition, it targets a potential mass market with what they believe would be a unique product. Initial sales forecasts outline that, with a national launch, production levels would be high enough to make Pet Offensive a cost effective proposition. The financial director (Adam Holland) has detailed to the Board that it would be unwise to expect Pet Offensive to make massive profits in its initial stages. The process whereby each contract or separate order from each supermarket would be individually negotiated means that the selling price of Pet Offensive will vary and so Adam also advises that contribution should be used as a basis for deciding whether or not to accept an order.

Adam has also used the estimated sales figures to produce a one year forecasted Profit and Loss Account and Balance Sheet assuming the launch of Pet Offensive was to proceed. Several key points have been raised:

● Final development costs, product testing for safety standards and national launch are estimated at a cost of £2.7 million. This would necessitate the raising of substantial funds. The projected financial plan has assumed that these funds could be raised by mortgaging Holland's land and buildings. Although other sources of funds would be available, Adam is aware of the resistance of his father and uncle to any further dilution of ownership.

● The company would need to use much of its liquid capital in order to purchase the materials required for production prior to the launch, coupled with the fact that Holland's supermarket clients often request extensive credit periods.

● Holland's has already invested £94,000 in the initial research and development of this idea and if the project does not proceed this cost would have to be written off.

To aid the board in their decision Adam has also used ratio analysis based upon his financial forecasts to assess the company's projected financial position. These indicate that although gearing would increase (to 40%) and liquidity fall (0.9 :1 on the acid test), performance ratios would improve – particularly the gross and net profit margins with a corresponding, though smaller, rise in the ROCE figure.

Adam's cousin Sarah (the personnel director) has criticised the financial forecast stating that forecasting sales in the fast-moving FMCG environment is of limited benefit. She has highlighted the fact that previous studies done with existing products have often proved to have little relationship to actual results.

Their alternative may be to sell the business outright and at least be able to leave a substantial sum of money for their families.

Appendix A **Sales Data for Holland Limited**

Year	Sales per year by % market value		Sales per year by % market volume	
	Air fresheners	Household polishers	Air fresheners	Household polishers
2000	17	11.2	8.4	13
2001	16.4	10.7	8.2	12.8
2002	14	10.3	7.8	12.5
Projected				
Year 1	12.7	9.9	7.6	12.3
Year 2	11.8	9.4	7.2	12
Year 3	11.1	8.6	6.7	11.8

1 **(a)** Outline the methods that Holland's Marketing and Sales department may have used to forecast the future sales figures of a new product like Pet Offensive. [8 marks]

(b) Evaluate the accuracy of Sarah's statement that 'forecasting sales in the FMCG environment is of limited benefit'. [12 marks]

2 **(a)** Analyse the merits of Adam's proposal to use contribution pricing as a strategy for this product. [10 marks]

(b) Discuss the effectiveness of ratio analysis in relation to Holland's as an aid to financial decision making. [10 marks]

DENNY'S ANSWERS

1 (a) Outline the methods that Holland's Marketing and Sales department may have used to forecast the future sales figures of a new product like Pet Offensive. **[8 marks]**

There are various methods available to a company like Holland's to forecast sales into the future. First, and probably one of the most popular techniques, is that Holland's could have used extrapolation. This is a method whereby the company takes its past sales figures for a number of years and plots them on a graph or chart. Then they use moving averages to iron out any erratic or seasonal factors that may have been contained in the data. This enables the company to establish a trend line and this line can then be extrapolated — extended into the future in order for the company to establish what sales may be at some future date. However, the problem with extrapolation is that past sales may not necessarily be a very good guide for the future. Anything may happen — external influences such as technological or legislative change would make the projected figures inaccurate.

Alternatively, the company could have used market research. This could be either primary or secondary. In the case of primary research, the company could have issued a questionnaire to a representative sample of customers and asked them questions such as 'how many' and 'how frequently would they buy the product' to give an idea of what sales may be like. Also a good method of primary research is a consumer taste panel as this is a form of qualitative research and would enable the company to find out consumer opinions and attitudes. With secondary research, also known as desk research, they could have used Government or industry/trade statistics to determine the size of the market. This is also useful research when trying to discover trends. However, market research is not always the best form of analysis. It must be done carefully and accurately, as it is easy to gain false information through biased questions or even an inaccurate method of sampling (non-representative).

As a final consideration Holland's could have used the Delphi technique. The company would get together a group of industry experts and ask their opinions on what the future sales will be. The panel would then use all their expertise, knowledge and experience to discuss the situation and arrive at a projected answer for the company. A criticism of this method, though, would be that it can prove expensive and often establishing the panel in the first place can be very difficult and time consuming.

$\frac{4}{8}$

How to score full marks

- The key to this question is to identify the **command word** and at what level it is directing you to respond (see page 5 for guidance on command words). In this instance the command word 'outline' indicates that your answer should be **explanatory.** Marks will be available for **Content (4 marks) and Application (4 marks),** and you are not required to analyse or evaluate (see page 6 for information on mark schemes and level-of-response marking).

- **At no stage in Denny's answer does he actually refer to Holland's situation. This makes it impossible for Denny to achieve any marks for application. His four marks are awarded purely on the basis of content.**

In the first paragraph Denny clearly and fluently describes the process of forecasting sales by extrapolation, but he needs **to put this in relation to Holland's situation.** He could have done this by saying that as Pet Offensive is a new and unique product and no previous sales data actually exists, extrapolation would have to be based on the sales figures of the closest available substitute. This would call into question the accuracy of any result obtained and would suggest that it was not advisable to use such a technique at all.

His second point is relevant in that market research would be a legitimate way of obtaining data for forecasting sales. In his explanation **Denny loses focus on the actual question** and digresses slightly into the pros and cons of market research. He could have gained **application marks** by suggesting that Holland's could have used a focus group of supermarket buyers to gauge their opinions, or by highlighting the fact that with a new and unique product, secondary research would have been of limited value.

In his last paragraph Denny should have related the Delphi technique much more closely to Holland's situation. Where would one find a panel of such experts for this product? Could Holland's afford the expense or even the time of gathering such a panel together? He could have suggested that the Delphi technique was not appropriate for Holland's as it is usually used to obtain long-range projections of market development rather than short-term sales forecasts which is what Holland's needed.

(b) Evaluate the accuracy of Sarah's statement that 'forecasting sales in the FMCG environment is of limited benefit'. [12 marks]

In my opinion Sarah is right. Fast-moving consumer goods are products with recognisable brand names in supermarkets and newsagents that have very high sales turnover. These goods are therefore selling regularly and frequently. Good examples are things like chocolate bars or washing powders. These are products that are usually made by well-known companies with lots of financial power and well-known brand names.

The main reason why I agree with Sarah is that because these products are in a highly competitive market, the companies that own them are always trying to get one up on each other. Branded products like these are always having advertising campaigns and special offers like 'buy one get one free', '33% extra free' or have promotional links to famous movies and such. This makes forecasting sales for one of these products virtually impossible, as you never know what your competitors are going to do next.

The case study describes how Holland's have suffered from a lot of new products being introduced by competitors in a FMCG market. Now Holland's want to introduce a new product. So the fact that there are frequently new products being released which would take away some, if not all, of your customers without you knowing about it first, makes forecasting sales in a way pointless. The forecast would be entirely inaccurate and probably out of date within a few weeks of it being done. This would mean that all the time and money that had been spent on forecasting sales, via whatever technique, would have been wasted, so causing unnecessary costs and thus reduced profits for the company.

In my judgement information is only useful if in the long run it generates more profit for the company than it costs the company to acquire the information in the first place. In my opinion information will only do this if it is useful, and in such a fast moving market as FMCGs information will only be useful for a very short period of time before a competitor does something to make it out of date. So I agree with Sarah — any benefits gained would be very short lived indeed.

(8/12)

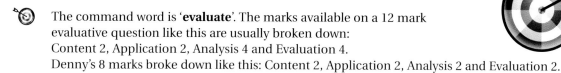

How to score full marks

The command word is '**evaluate**'. The marks available on a 12 mark evaluative question like this are usually broken down:
Content 2, Application 2, Analysis 4 and Evaluation 4.
Denny's 8 marks broke down like this: Content 2, Application 2, Analysis 2 and Evaluation 2.

Denny's answer achieved the full allocation of marks for content and application. **He raised several relevant points and applied them directly to the FMCG market and the situation of Holland's**. Denny's first paragraph defining an FMCG product, although repetitive, would earn him some marks for content. His line of reasoning in the rest of his response is not about the pros and cons of forecasting in general (a common line of argument many students would take in response to this question) but specifically about forecasting in fast moving markets.

Denny also **uses information from the case study to support his argument**. Note he does not copy out text but refers to the situation in general. **This is exactly what is required to achieve application marks**.

There are, however, several problems with Denny's answer. Firstly, it is one-sided – it concentrates solely on reasons why he supports Sarah's statement. **There are usually two viewpoints to any business problem** and Denny's one-sidedness makes it difficult for the answer to achieve the full 4 marks for analysis. This then has a knock-on effect for evaluation marks, as it is impossible to achieve top marks for demonstrating well-reasoned and sound judgement if you have only considered one side of the argument.

To achieve full marks, it would be necessary also to consider the benefits of sales forecasting even in such a fast moving market. The main areas that could be addressed would be:

● Even a forecast that is only accurate for a short period of time can provide essential information to the business so that it can plan staffing, production levels and raw material purchases, thus avoiding problems associated with over- or under-stocking of goods.

● Forecasting sales is essential if the business wishes to undertake any other budgetary exercises such as cashflow forecasts. In Holland's case some projected figures are likely to be a definite requirement if they wish to approach external organisations like a bank for finance.

● Sales forecasts can also be used in conjunction with target setting and motivational aspects, thus helping the business to become more efficient and hopefully profitable overall.

In order to achieve full marks for evaluation, key judgements need to be made. A suitable argument here would be that as Pet Offensive appears to be entering a unique market, there are no competitors whose actions need to be taken into account at first and so, despite the limitations of forecasting in a FMCG market, this makes any forecasts made more realistic. Even if forecasts are inaccurate or accurate only for a limited period, it is better to have some indication of what the likely level of sales and demand will be when launching a brand new product, rather than no indication at all.

2 (a) Analyse the merits of Adam's proposal to use contribution pricing as a strategy for this product. [10 marks]

Contribution is when the company adds up all the variable costs involved in making the product, such as labour and raw materials, and then sets the selling price at a level higher than this. The idea here is that as long as the price received is greater than the total variable costs, then the company will make a positive contribution. This is given by the formula:

Contribution = Selling price − Variable costs.

This contribution is used first of all to pay off the fixed costs of the business and then, after all fixed costs have been paid, to start making a profit. The theory goes that so long as a positive contribution is being received, it is worthwhile selling the product, as some contribution is better than none. The more contributions that are made, the faster fixed costs are covered and thus eventually the greater the level of profits.

I think this would be a suitable method for Holland's to employ for this product. Firstly, because the product is going to be taking advantage of existing manufacturing facilities that are also used to produce other products such as air fresheners, it would be unfair to include these <u>fixed costs</u> or overheads in the cost of producing Pet Offensive as in actuality they are shared. Including fixed costs as well would be using a method of cost-plus pricing. Thus, so long as Pet Offensive is making a contribution toward these running costs, as it would by definition already be covering its variable costs, it would be providing benefits to the company and eventually profits.

Secondly, although Holland's is struggling, according to the case study, it does not actually say they are making a loss. Therefore, I would assume that Holland's existing products are already doing sufficiently well to generate some profit (although weakening) and so fixed costs must be being covered already. Therefore, if the company is able to sell the new product with a positive contribution, virtually all of this would be pure additional profits and so be benefiting the company. Similarly as a new product, as Adam says, it may be unwise to expect it to make huge profits straight away. So perhaps the idea of it just making a contribution toward the business, whilst being supported by Holland's more well known products, would be a wise decision, while the company waits for their new product to become established.

However, the fact that it is new is an important point. Usually a new product entering the market would use some form of promotional pricing strategy. I think in this case Holland's should use a penetration pricing policy. This is where the company would set the price of Pet Offensive deliberately low, perhaps even making a loss, to try to gain a foothold in the market and gain market share. In the short term this could lose Holland's money. However, it would help them to attract customers away from competitors and back to themselves and in the long term, when they raise prices to normal levels, they would have an established customer base. A benefit of this is that if the customers like this new product they may even be attracted to Holland's other products and start to purchase those as well. Thus although, I think, contribution pricing is fine I would probably advise the company to use penetration pricing as this is a new product and it needs to gain a foothold.

9/10

How to score full marks

- This is very good answer. Denny **considers both sides of the argument**. The mark scheme for this analytical question would be:
  Content 2, Application 3 and Analysis 5 in two levels of response.
  Denny's 9 marks break down: Content 2, Application 3 and Analysis 4.

- Denny gives a comprehensive definition of what contribution pricing is and how it is calculated along with supporting formula. This is a classic way of approaching an AS question. Unfortunately, at A2 this is regarded as just textbook knowledge and only receives content marks. **It is vital to remember that at A2 the focus, and the marks, is on the higher order skills of analysis and evaluation**. Denny's first paragraph would therefore earn him 2 marks for content.

- Paragraph two may seem a bit brief but Denny has made a very good three-stage argument about the reason why contribution pricing would be suitable and **places his answer in context**. He then follows this up in the next paragraph with **a further well-developed line of reasoning still relating directly to the specific circumstances of the company and product**.

- Finally, to make this a very good response, Denny **considers a relevant alternative**: penetration pricing. Once again he discusses in detail why, in the context of the product, he feels penetration pricing would be a suitable alternative. **The consideration of both sides of the argument, coupled with the constant reference to the specific scenario, gains Denny top marks for application and almost full marks for analysis as well**.

- The reason Denny missed out on full marks for analysis is that with Pet Offensive having a USP and therefore no competition, a much better strategy would probably be price skimming, that is setting as high a price as the market will allow and making as much profit as possible.

- An alternative, and more focused line to examine, would be reasons why contribution pricing may not be a suitable basis. Contribution pricing does not allow the company to take advantage of prevailing market conditions. It can be difficult to classify some costs into fixed and variable components – this means that contribution pricing can have some degree of inaccuracy built in.

(b) Discuss the effectiveness of ratio analysis in relation to Holland's as an aid to financial decision making. [10 marks]

Ratio analysis can be effective and ineffective in helping decision making. Ratio analysis is the process whereby a business uses numerical information to assess its financial performance and financial stability by comparing one piece of financial information with another, for example, last year's accounts, a competitor's accounts or, as in this case, forecast accounts. These are the key points.

ADVANTAGES

- Ratio analysis is quantitative analysis, therefore it gives definite measurable results that can be used to assess performance or, in this case, projected performance. In this way they actually provide a concrete basis for making decisions, that is, they are numbers and the directors can look at them and decide if they are any good or not. For example, the board of directors can see that although gearing has increased, the company would still be regarded as being low geared at 40%. This helps the directors make the decision that it may not be as much of a risk as it would first appear.

- Ratios can also be used to assess areas of strength and weakness, that is, the forecasted results show that there should be an increase in performance/profitability ratios — this would indicate that the decision should proceed. However, the results also show that the company would become illiquid (from the acid test). This though could be an advantage since the company have projected this in advance, so they can take steps to ensure that even with this position, it doesn't become a problem. They could make sure debtors pay up in time, or they could extend payment periods to suppliers. Alternatively, they could increase gearing even further and therefore hold more cash so that this problem never actually occurs.

DISADVANTAGES

- The ratios are based on historical figures and therefore are no guide to the future.

- They are only as accurate as the information provided.

- They don't take into account external factors or qualitative factors.

EVALUATION

Although there are some limitations to ratios it is better to have some information when making decisions than none at all. Therefore they are definitely of some value to the company.

6/10

- Denny has obviously not left enough time for the final part of this question and so attempts to gain marks quickly by mentioning as many disadvantages as he can think of and making a throw-away line on evaluation at the end.

- **Level-of-response marking (see page 6) means that you receive more marks as your arguments develop depth and demonstrate understanding of business relationships.** Although Denny's list is all relevant, there is only brief and limited development of each point. This makes it extremely hard for Denny to get past level 1 on analysis or evaluation. Denny would have done better not to have wasted time at the beginning defining and explaining ratio analysis, and to have **focused instead on developing one of his list of disadvantages into a fully analytical argument.**

- **The command word 'discuss' makes clear this question needs an evaluative response.** The 10 marks would be allocated: Content 1, Application 3, Analysis 3 and Evaluation 3. Denny's 6 marks were awarded: Content 1, Application 2, Analysis 2 and Evaluation 1.

- **The way to approach this question would have been to provide a balanced argument giving reasons for both sides of the argument and then to propose a carefully thought-out conclusion relating to Holland's situation.**

- Denny gains virtually all of his marks in the two extended paragraphs under the heading 'advantages'. In these paragraphs he has used good exam technique. He has considered two reasons why ratio analysis would be useful to a company in Holland's position. **He not only proposes theoretical approaches as to why it could prove helpful, but also uses the financial information from the case study to discuss exact situations where and when it could help with the decision facing the company.** In this way Denny is gaining marks for analysis, application and evaluation. The evaluation mark is gained by Denny making a judgement regarding the acid test figures and proposing a reasonable solution to the problem they present.

- **Denny would have gained top level analysis marks if he had taken the same approach in his disadvantages section.** An interesting point to note here though is that this analysis is not being undertaken on historical figures but on projected figures. This is an important aspect for generating some good evaluation. As Denny states, ratio analysis is only as good as the information provided, and in this case the information is based on a sales forecast in a FMCG market, which can be considered as being highly inaccurate.

- A final point that could be made is that in a situation like Holland's, one vital piece of information would be a forecasted cashflow, especially given the fall in liquidity expressed and the outlined problems of obtaining stocks.

Don't forget ...

You may well be required to perform calculations on this paper. These may be for either marketing or finance. **The only real way to revise practical applications is to practise them.**

Make sure you leave enough time to answer all the questions fully. Very few marks are available at A2 for providing textbook definitions.

To get top level marks on many case study questions, it is necessary to relate your answers to the context of the business and the scenario given. **Think about how situations would affect the individual business you are given**.

The information in the case study is there to help you. In many case studies there will be supporting charts or tables of data. Pay particular attention to these as they may provide valuable clues about market trends, competition or costs and revenues.

Remember business studies topics are interrelated, particularly marketing and finance. For example, sales forecasts are used to determine the basis for cashflow forecasts and the business's productive activity, which determines costs.

Know the meaning of the key command words and look at the mark allocation. For AQA candidates, **the majority of questions in the case study exam will always require you to analyse and evaluate**. This is a skill that you need to develop through practice.

To gain high marks in questions that are marked through level-of-response marking, **try to develop one or two in-depth arguments rather than a series of superficial points**. Levels of response mean that as your arguments gain more insight and depth you move into higher mark bands (see page 6). If you don't expand upon relevant points you will not be able to move into the higher response levels for each question.

Real-life experience can be just as useful as classroom knowledge. Taking part in Young Enterprise schemes or obtaining literature from banks can be a valuable way of building your insight into marketing and finance processes.

You don't have to answer questions in the order they are set. As long as you clearly identify on your script which question it is you are answering, play to your own strengths and first answer the questions where you feel you have the best knowledge.

Market analysis

Extrapolation is a statistical process of forecasting sales based on historical data. It involves the use of moving averages to eradicate erratic results and seasonal effects to produce a smooth predicted trend line. It is usually represented on a graph.

- A three-year moving average is calculated by taking the sum of three year's sales figures, finding the average and then plotting this point for the middle year. This is then repeated for subsequent sets of data.

Year	Sales (£000s)	Calculation	Three-year moving average
1999	212		
2000	216	(212 + 216 + 220) / 3	216
2001	220	(216 + 220 + 227) / 3	221
2002	227		

However, past events and trends are no guarantee of the future, especially in rapidly changing environments, so extrapolated results could be inaccurate.

Correlation shows the existence of a causal link between two variables. For example, there usually exists a positive causal link between advertising expenditure and sales, as expenditure increases so do sales. A negative causal link for an inferior product could be that, as income rises, sales fall.

Asset-led versus market-led
- **Asset-led marketing** bases the marketing strategy, tactics and decisions on the firm's existing strengths in consideration of customer requirements. This approach maximises the chances of a firm's success as it joins the concepts of what customers want with what it is capable of delivering. Asset-led companies may turn down potential opportunities if they don't fit their strengths.
- **Market-led companies** base their strategy and marketing decisions on customer requirements. These help to ensure success by producing what customers want. The disadvantage is that companies may diversify into areas where they are comparatively weak, with little expertise.

Marketing strategy

Marketing strategy is the company's medium- to long-term plan to enable it to meets its marketing objectives (covered in AQA AS level). Marketing strategies involve choices between:
- Mass versus niche markets
- Product differentiation versus low-cost cheap price
- Local, regional, national or international targeting
- The four components of Ansoff's matrix:
  - Market penetration
  - Product development
  - Market development
  - Diversification

The marketing model is a scientific framework for making marketing decisions. It consists of five stages:
- Setting marketing objectives in consideration of the company objectives and mission statement
- Market research – the gathering of data such as: market value and volume, competition and consumer profiles
- Form hypotheses – plans on how to effectively achieve the set objectives
- Hypothesis testing – through further research, product trials and test marketing
- Evaluation – review of the success or failure of the process actually undertaken

Marketing planning

Marketing planning is the detailed analysis of how a company intends to implement its marketing strategy to achieve its objectives. It concerns the:

- **Marketing mix to be used** – detailed tactics of price, place, promotion and product and the co-ordination of activities throughout the company.
- **Marketing budget** – targets and the amount of funds available to achieve them. This should be set in line with:
  - The objectives to be achieved
  - The size of expected sales
  - The firm's financial position
  - Competitor actions
  - State of the economy

The budgetary process can also be used as a motivator through delegation and consultation.

- **Sales forecasting** – the methods of forecasting sales include:
  - **Extrapolation** (see above)
  - **Market research** – primary or secondary research into consumer buying habits, trends and market size to try to establish expected levels of sales
  - **The Delphi technique** – consultation with industry experts over their expectations for market developments. Usually used for long-term projections.
  - **Management experience**, market knowledge and hunches or the experience and knowledge of their sales force.

Company accounts

- **Capital expenditure** is the money spent by companies in the procurement of fixed assets (tangible or intangible) and as such affects the balance sheet position of the firm. Capital expenditure is matched to yearly revenue generation through the process of depreciation.
- **Revenue expenditure** is the money used by the firm in its day-to-day expenses. It is the finance used to assist the business in the generation of sales. In this respect it includes all expense items, purchases and financial charges, e.g. interest.

A **profit and loss account** is a financial statement that examines a company's financial performance over a period of time, usually one year. It is a measure of the firm's revenues against its costs resulting in either a profit or loss. Key areas for analysis consist of profit quality and profit utilisation.

Profit quality – high quality profit is regarded as being profit from repeatable sources, i.e. it can be accessed again and again and signals the possibility of likely future success. Low quality profit is derived from a one-off event, such as arising from the sale of assets or subsidiaries, i.e. it cannot be accessed again.

A **balance sheet** is a financial statement detailing the assets and liabilities held by a business. It examines the financial strength of a business by contrasting what a business owns with what it owes, i.e. what the company has and where the money came from. Its primary use is in assessing the business's worth and financial stability through ratios such as gearing and the acid test (see below).

However, it must be noted that profit and loss accounts only contain historical, quantifiable data. They do not show market and/or product developments, expertise, experience or the motivation levels of the workforce. Similarly the data within them may often be '**window dressed**' – artificially manipulated to present the business in a better light. An example of this would be the overvaluing of intangible assets such as brand names to make the balance sheet appear stronger.

Working capital is the difference between the business short term assets (current assets) and its short term debts (current liabilities). It is a measure of the day-to-day finances available for the running of the firm and is used to pay running costs such as expenses and purchases. It is given by the formula:

Current assets – Current liabilities

Working capital has implications for the liquidity of the business. Too little liquidity and the company may face problems meeting its daily running costs; too much and it may be incurring an opportunity cost of investing the funds more effectively. Exam questions are frequently asked on methods and implications of improving working capital such as: reducing debtor periods, extending supplier credit, sale and lease back of assets, use of long-term liabilities like loans or reduction in outflows (costs).

Depreciation is the method by which the capital expenditure on a fixed asset is distributed to the profit and loss account of the period of the asset's useful life. It is calculated by using the formula:

$$\text{Annual depreciation charge} = \frac{\text{Cost of the asset} - \text{Residual (resale or scrap) value}}{\text{Asset's useful lifetime}}$$

Depreciation is regarded as being a provision – it does not involve a real movement of cash nor is it a method of saving for a future replacement asset – it is a bookkeeping entry only. It is charged as an expense on the profit and loss and written off the value of the asset recorded on the balance sheet. The key effects are:
- reducing the level of reported profits
- reducing the balance sheet valuations.

Ratio analysis

The focus at A2 is on the understanding and interpretation of ratios rather than calculation. You will not be supplied formula so you must learn them and their categories. A comprehensive list of ratios and their interpretation can be found in any A2 textbook.

Areas to be considered:
- Liquidity ratios   – For AQA candidates this is the acid test only
- Financial efficiency – Asset turnover, stock turnover and debtor days
- Gearing
- Profitability   – Net profit margin, gross profit margin and ROCE
- Shareholders ratios – Dividend per share and dividend yield
- To be able to present balanced arguments regarding ratio analysis results you must also consider the limitations of this form of financial analysis.

Contribution and break-even analysis

Break-even analysis is covered in *Do Brilliantly AS Business Studies*.

Contribution is the difference between a product's selling price and its total variable costs and is given by the formula:

    Contribution per unit = Individual product selling price – Total variable costs per product

or

    Total contribution = Total product sales revenue – Total variable costs

It can also be used as a quick way to calculate profits at different levels of output and sales. This is done using the formula:

    Profit = Total contribution – Fixed costs

Contribution can also be helpful with decision-making. The general rule is that as long as a product is making a positive level of contribution it is worth continuing production or accepting an order (even at a lower than normal price), as the additional contribution made will either help the business pay fixed costs or generate extra profit.

Investment decision-making

This involves the examination of possible investments using investment appraisal techniques. These are the main techniques:

Payback is a simple technique that calculates how long an investment takes to return its initial cost and uses the formula:

Payback period = Number of full years investment not paid by revenue generated
+ (Investment left to pay/Revenue generated next year)

It is quick, simple and easy but does not take into account the real value of money over time nor does it calculate profits made by alternative investment.

Average rate of return (ARR) is an appraisal technique that measures the average level of profits made by an investment. It uses the formula:

$$\text{Average rate of return} = \frac{\text{Average annual profit from investment}}{\text{Cost of the investment}}$$

This allows comparisons of profit to be made between investment choices. However, it does not calculate payback time and only compares average profits not total profits made. This method also does not take into account the real value of money over time.

Net present value is a method of discounted cash flow, i.e. it does take into account the way the real value of money will drop over time through inflation. This is done by discounting future cash inflows to their apparent worth at today's value of money through the application of discount factors. The sum of cash inflows for each project is found and the initial investment cost removed. The project with the highest net present value result is regarded as being the most worthwhile in financial terms.

Net present value is complex to calculate and it is difficult to choose the correct discount rate.

Limitations

All investment appraisal techniques require forecasted figures and so are subject to inaccuracies. They also only consider financial implications of investments. They make no allowance for qualitative factors such as:

Environmental and ethical issues   – Pollution and use of non-sustainable resources
Industrial relations   – Replacement of workforce by machines
Corporate image   – Some profitable projects may well reflect badly on the business.

Question to try

The question to try on marketing and finance can be found in the integrated case study question to try at the end of Chapter 2 (page 37). This mirrors the actual examination requirements of AQA A2 paper 4.

Expansive Management

Chris Grogan was one of those managers who are larger than life – always full of energy and enthusiasm and driving himself forward with a commitment to work that made it obvious he would succeed.

Chris got his first break fourteen years ago when, fresh from college, he secured a job working on the docks at Great Yarmouth for a timber importing company. It was here he got his first taste of cranes. Not everyone is suited to working up to several hundred feet in the air on their own but Chris loved it and so a passion was born.

Three years later he became a sales advisor for Stensons Ltd. one of the UK's largest crane manufacturers and suppliers. Chris got the position due to his already extensive knowledge of different cranes, their capabilities, strengths and weaknesses. In this aspect he proved invaluable to the directors of Stensons by providing advice and recommendations for product improvement and also the easy manner with which he was able to discuss technicalities with customers and manufacturing employees alike. Within four years Chris had joined the management and on the retirement of the existing Sales Director (Claire Lake), two years ago, Chris was invited to take the position, which he readily accepted.

Eighteen months ago Chris approached the rest of the board with the proposition that they were missing out on a huge opportunity – that of the European market. Chris had thought this through and done some initial investigations. His actual proposal was that to maintain a European sales force would be too expensive. But, if the company could increase manufacturing capability and produce more cranes, then these could be leased to a network of European agents already established as sales and hire outlets across Europe.

Following further investigations by all the various departments it has been decided to proceed. An expansion plan has been drawn up which would involve building a new factory for the increased production at Crawley, 12 miles away, and also the recruitment and training of employees. A list of activities required and their duration times has been drawn up, see Appendix A. The board also see this an opportunity to introduce some new CAD/CAM and information technology communication systems into the manufacturing process and organisation as a whole.

Ben Goffin, the Personnel Director, is concerned about the impact the expansion could have on certain aspects of his human resource management function. He estimates that the new factory could effectively double the number of employees to nearly 800. He is also concerned that the new factory will be on a separate site and that the excellent informal links that exist between management and employees could be lost. Currently, Stensons use a system of informal discussion groups to raise and solve problems whenever they arise. Stensons prides itself on being a family run firm with family values, including towards its workforce. Ben feels that with an expanded operation and the need to maintain excellent communication links between departments such as manufacturing, purchasing, delivery and finance, perhaps some of the informality may be lost and a more formal participation system imposed to maintain good communications.

Ben has outlined his particular concern that during the implementation stage and start of the new factory it is paramount that the whole of Stensons' employee base is operating as a team. With the expanded workforce, careful planning of the whole operation such as recruitment training and arranging working spaces will need to be carried out, otherwise the whole new factory may become a disaster.

Appendix A

Proposed new factory network data

Activity letter	Activity	Preceded by	Duration (months)
A	Architectural designs	–	12
B	Planning approval	A	8
C	Order materials	B	6
D	Lay foundations	B	6
E	Building framework	C and D	24
F	Interior fixtures and fittings	B	4
G	Installation of machinery	F and H	12
H	Recruitment and staff training	B	34

1 (a) Outline the communication problems that may arise as a result of the proposed expansion. [8 marks]

(b) Recommend how Stensons could maintain the level of employee involvement as the business expands. [12 marks]

2 (a) Construct Stensons' network diagram showing the earliest start times and latest finish times of every activity. State the critical path for the new factory project. [10 marks]

(b) Discuss the case for/against the use of computer technology in a manufacturing business. [10 marks]

JENNY'S ANSWERS

1 (a) Outline the communication problems that may arise as a result of the
proposed expansion.

[8 marks]

Poor communications could arise at Stensons for many reasons. Firstly, there would be many more employees, quite a lot of whom would be new. The increased number of employees could mean wider spans of control for managers, meaning less management time per employee, thus less communication would take place.

Secondly, just the increase in numbers could mean it takes much longer for messages and instructions to get around, so slowing down the whole process.

Finally, if all the new employees are on the new site and the old employees are on the existing site this could cause a 'them and us' attitude between the sites and promote poor communication between the two. If, however, the sites are combined this could cause resentment and a decline in motivation among the original workforce due to the break-up of familiar work groups and social groups. Poor communications could again result as employees become demotivated and less inclined to cooperate with managers.

A final point could be difficulties with foreign agents and language barriers, meaning that orders are miscommunicated or misinterpreted and the wrong goods are delivered or, even worse, manufactured from scratch. This could cost the company a lot of money.

8/8

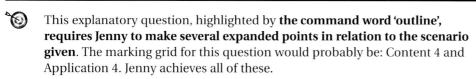

How to score full marks

  This explanatory question, highlighted by **the command word 'outline',**
requires Jenny to make several expanded points in relation to the scenario
given. The marking grid for this question would probably be: Content 4 and
Application 4. Jenny achieves all of these.

Jenny has been very successful in putting her answer in context. Jenny has made four
relevant points and developed each one in the direct context of the expansion of the
factory. She has also included references to the idea of communication problems with a
new site, new employees and overseas connections.

The line of reasoning that outlines the possible reactions and repercussions from deciding
whether or not the existing workforce is split between the two sites, is a particularly relevant
one.

(b) Recommend how Stensons could maintain the level of employee involvement as the business expands. [12 marks]

I think that the personnel guy is probably right and that Stensons will no longer be able to continue as the nice family run business with informal discussions. The business will essentially become too big for this to be the case and if they do try to keep this they may find that a lot of messages get lost, forgotten or miscommunicated. There would be increasing costs and waste and clients' deliveries could be forgotten or late. This would possibly lose Stensons profit and clients, and word could spread that Stensons were unreliable.

I therefore think it is imperative that Stensons do try to maintain communicative efficiency throughout the organisation. A business cannot reach its full potential and achieve success if it suffers from poor communication. Stensons could achieve this in various ways. First, they could make their informal discussion groups more formal and use workers councils. These are where management meet with the workers' elected representatives to discuss any problems or issues that might have arisen lately. These take place on a regular basis such as weekly or fortnightly so that not too long a period of time should have passed before any problem that has occurred gets a chance to be discussed.

Alternatively, the company could introduce quality circles. This may be a better option as nearly everybody would get to participate in these whereas with workers councils it is just elected representatives. But also these would be better as quality circles involve a range of people from different departments and levels in each group. In this way Stensons could merge people from the different sites in the same quality circle grouping and thus improve inter-site and interdepartmental communications. After all, it says in the case study that the new site at Crawley is only 12 miles away so really this shouldn't be too much of a problem. The company could provide special buses once a week to allow people to attend their groups. Quality circles would also bring additional benefits like helping to solve production problems or suggestions of ideas for improvements. Quality circles therefore would not only improve communications but would also improve motivation as workers would believe they had a chance to show their abilities and solve problems and thus receive recognition from the management. This then would encourage employees to participate and continue participating, especially if Stensons introduced a reward system for ideas as well.

How to score full marks

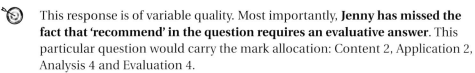

This response is of variable quality. Most importantly, **Jenny has missed the fact that 'recommend' in the question requires an evaluative answer**. This particular question would carry the mark allocation: Content 2, Application 2, Analysis 4 and Evaluation 4.
Her 8 marks are awarded as follows: Content 2, Application 2, Analysis 3 and Evaluation 1.

Jenny's first paragraph is entirely irrelevant. She is not actually answering the question asked which is how might employee involvement be maintained; she is actually stating why she agrees that it can't be. **This gains no marks as Jenny is answering what she thinks is the question, not what the question actually is.**

In the second paragraph, Jenny raises the idea of works councils, which she refers to as workers councils. This is a method by which communication levels and employee involvement could be maintained. **Unfortunately, in this instance, Jenny just describes what they are.** She offers no development as to how they could maintain employee involvement or their advantages and disadvantages – so this is just a **content** point with no **application** marks.

Her second suggestion of quality circles is much better developed. Here Jenny describes what they are, how they operate, why they might be better than works councils (achieving a mark for evaluation) and the benefits the company and employees receive. She relates this answer to the problem of having two sites, thus putting it in context as well. To achieve full marks **Jenny needed to follow the same evaluative style** with her point about works councils or have raised other ideas such as introducing teamworking or employee shareholder schemes. Jenny finishes her answer by placing her response within the focus of the question about how involvement could be maintained.

The key to structuring a good evaluative answer to this question is to start with the method which, in your opinion, would achieve the best level of participation and involvement and explain why, given the context of expanding operations and split-site manufacturing.

2 (a) Construct Stensons' network diagram showing the earliest start times and latest finish times of every activity. State the critical path for the new factory project.

[10 marks]

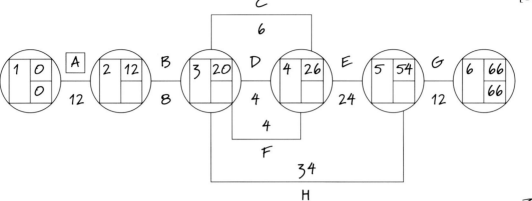

The critical path would be A, B, H, G.

How to score full marks

This is a good answer although Jenny has not completed the diagram. She has drawn it clearly and accurately labelled all the component parts. Unfortunately she has not completed the latest finishing time boxes. Although Jenny has missed one of the areas asked for, she still receives a high mark for this question as the examiner can identify that Jenny has a relatively good knowledge and understanding of this topic. Jenny has made sure that:

- No lines cross.
- She has included a starting and finishing node.
- All activities are clearly labelled and show duration.

Jenny receives: 5 marks for drawing and labelling the network, 2 marks for calculating earliest start times and 1 mark for identifying the critical path.

Jenny has correctly identified the critical path and also receives merit for this. The critical path is the activities which have no spare float time. If these activities overrun the whole project would be delayed.

A model answer is given below.

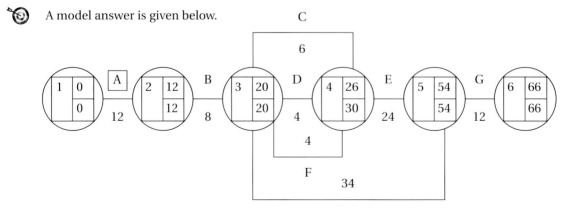

(b) Discuss the case for/against the use of computer technology in a manufacturing business. [10 marks]

Computers can be very useful in a business, be it a manufacturing organisation or not. In this case it is a manufacturing company and so they can use computers for communication and CAD/CAM systems. CAD/CAM systems would be really good as this would enable the new factory to design and build its cranes cost effectively and quicker than more traditional processes. The use of automatic equipment and robots in manufacture would also speed up production and save the company money on labour. I would imagine that this would be quite a large cost saving as labour for crane manufacture would probably have to be highly skilled in some areas. In this instance, the introduction of this technology would not cause major demotivation through people being replaced by robots and redundancies taking place as the company are expanding and creating more jobs at the same time, so really there should be no problem from the workforce. The most significant drawback for the company will actually be the cost of training existing workers to use the new equipment or perhaps even finding new employees who already possess the right skills. There can't be that many CAD/CAM trained crane designers out there. This would no doubt mean that probably new employees would require training. Perhaps this is why on the network diagram it takes 34 weeks to recruit and train employees. This would be roughly 10 or 11 months so I guess the company has already thought about this and made allowances.

In this case then, I can see no real problems introducing computer technology, as given enough time they can either recruit or train employees to use it and there should be no resistance as the company is increasing jobs at the same time. It might prove difficult to teach some old dogs new tricks, but those people who are resistant to change should be a minority and as the whole project takes two years anyway quite a lot of these people could be lost through natural wastage.

7/10

How to score full marks

- A question of this type again requires evaluation and the marks would be awarded: Content 1, Application 3, Analysis 3 and Evaluation 3.

- Jenny's 7 marks would be awarded: Content 1, Application 2, Analysis 2 and Evaluation 2.

- Although Jenny's answer is detailed, **highly relevant to the case study and contains evaluative arguments and statements, there is actually only one point that has been discussed.** This makes achieving top marks difficult. In her opening sentences, Jenny actually identifies that computer technology could mean **computers for communication** as well as CAD/CAM systems. It states this in the case study as well. Unfortunately, Jenny has become so involved in CAD/CAM systems that she forgets to discuss computers for communication.

- This is why **it is important to break down your answer into new paragraphs every time you are starting a new point or demonstrating a new skill.** Had Jenny done this, it would have been apparent at a quick glance that she had actually only developed a single argument. **Her reasoning, judgements and sense of application are all very good but without examining several lines of approach she cannot achieve top marks.**

Don't forget ...

Make sure you leave enough time to answer the final question on the integrated case study, as this will usually be worth the most marks (usually 20). You don't have to answer questions in the order that they are set. The final question will often be worth up to 25% of the total paper. By leaving insufficient time to answer you are severely limiting your chances of a high overall grade.

Use the information given in the scenario as a prompt to help you. The information in the text and appendices is there for a reason.

Although questions may be about operations management, don't be afraid to draw on other areas. In question 2 (b) for example, a good well-developed human resource argument about motivation and productive efficiency would have been a reasonable line to take.

Stay focused on the question, particularly questions with higher mark allocations. Students often become wrapped up in their own arguments and actually forget what question it is they're meant to be answering. Re-read the question after each paragraph you write so you stay focused.

Don't use bullet pointed lists or a plan layout when trying to gain marks if short of time. Usually an extended piece of prose will take less time to write and actually gain you more marks as you develop a relevant point and move through the response levels.

Always try to make your answers refer to the circumstances of the business or situation you have been presented with. Marks are always available for context or application. Alongside this, it makes achieving higher order evaluation marks easier as you can then make a specific reasoned judgement about the most important areas that influence or impact upon the scenario given.

Keep up to date with business issues in the media. As business studies is a real-life subject whose theories are actually developed and applied by managers every day, being able to select and use a real-life example to add weight to your responses will help boost both your understanding of the dynamic business world, and consequently your grades as well.

Presentation is important. All examination papers now carry marks available for quality of language, i.e. these assess your ability to use terminology and language clearly and appropriately. In particular, the use of well-structured paragraphs is a good way to demonstrate to the examiner that you are about to discuss a new point or employ a different examination skill, e.g. you have now moved from analysing to evaluating.

When revising particular theories or applications for 'People and operations management' make sure you learn not just the theory itself but also advantages and criticisms. Very few things in business studies are absolutes and you need to be able to express both sides of an argument.

Communication

For a business to be successful it needs good communication. Management style will have a large influence on the type and effectiveness of communication. Democratic organisations particularly need excellent two-way communication systems. The speed and accuracy of communication is also controlled to some degree by the organisational structure of the company. These are AQA AS topics that should be reviewed for this unit.

Communication influences – Good communication increases morale and motivation. Effective communication allows processes such as delegation and participation to be implemented and used. It secures employees, i.e. they know what they are doing, are more motivated and correspondingly more productive. Good communication also provides better information faster, allowing improved management decision-making. Overall though good communication makes sure the business is co-ordinated and working towards the same objectives and goals.

Barriers to communication can exist in an organisational set-up that blocks the use of effective communication. These barriers may be:
- **Attitudes** – Management styles may be autocratic, employee relations may develop 'them and us' mentalities or there may be lack of awareness. Managers may be unaware that some employees are excluded from communication networks.
- **Language** – Different language usage between senior and shop floor staff, or the use of complex and difficult to understand technical terms.
- **Compatibility** – Not all employees may have the same IT equipment (especially in a large organisation) therefore some employees cannot effectively 'talk' to each other.
- **Communication overload** – Too much information can lead to the key points of messages, instructions or objectives being missed by subordinate employees. This then leads to a lack of coordination.
- **Distance** – In a large hierarchical organisation, the distance between the sender and receiver may cause communications to be slowed or distorted as they pass through levels. This makes confirmation of understanding and obtaining feedback difficult.

Use of IT
Advantages
- Access to huge data sources via MIS systems or intra/internets
- Improved communication links and speed of communications with remote points – can help with cost reductions
- Improved information to customers – through publicity materials and websites

Disadvantages
- Cost – equipment and training and the need for frequent upgrades
- Compatibility (see above). It is also very difficult for a large organisation to provide every employee with a new computer or new software at exactly the same time.
- Loss of face-to-face interaction can be demotivating for employees and deter some customers.

Employer/employee relations

This concerns the main area of the attitudes and working relationships between managers and employees.

Individual versus collective bargaining
- **Individual bargaining** is when each employee separately negotiates his or her pay and working conditions.
- **Collective bargaining** is the negotiation of pay and conditions between managers and representatives of their employees, usually by trade unions. Agreements reached are binding on the whole workforce. Collective bargaining provides advantages in that it is quicker and easier to negotiate with one body rather than with many. This saves the business time and money and also ends with one system to implement. The disadvantage is that collectively the workers hold more influence and power than as individuals, and so may well be able to negotiate better deals (such as pay increases) than may have been the case as individuals, increasing running costs.

Employee participation and industrial democracy

Employee participation considers the aspect of involving employees in the process of business decision-making and the methods by which this is achieved.

- **Works councils** – A meeting/discussion forum between managers and employees to discuss issues like conditions, pay and generate ideas for improving to the factory. Employees are represented by elected members.
- **Employee shareholders** – Allowing employees to purchase shares in the business to encourage motivation and performance as they now hold a financial stake in the company. The company itself can also gain tax concessions from the Inland Revenue.
- **Autonomous work groups** – This is a team of workers who are given the power to decide what is the best way to complete a given task. It is a process of decentralised teamworking, They are able to elect their own team leader and decide to some degree on the allocation and use of resources. This encourages motivation through trust and achievement. However, to operate autonomously employees require training, which can be costly.
- **Teamworking** – The collection of workers into supporting groups rather than individual processes or units. It is considered that teamworking provides several benefits:
  - Motivation through achievement of social and esteem needs
  - Reduced levels in the hierarchy and improve communication
  - Allows employees to support each other and develop each other's strengths and obviate weaknesses through working together.

Trade Unions and ACAS

Trade unions are organisations of workers that represent the interests of their membership. Their mission is to protect and improve the economic and working conditions of their members. This includes areas such as: pay negotiations (see collective bargaining); achieving a healthier and safer working environment, job security and representing members in case of disputes. Trade unions can use a variety of industrial actions in the event of negotiations failing. These are:

- **Overtime bans** – The refusal by employees to work longer than contracted hours, perhaps causing the company to miss delivery dates or have to hire more employees raising costs
- **Go slows** – A deliberate policy of working slowly, reducing productivity and thus affecting costs and profits
- **Work to rule** – Employees refuse to undertake any activities that is not part of the terms of their employment contract
- **Strikes** – The withdrawal of the employees labour from the organisations premises, often accompanied by picketing actions

Trade unions do offer benefits to organisations (see collective bargaining above).

ACAS is the Advisory, Conciliation and Arbitration Service. Its role is to act as an independent organisation and help to resolve industrial disputes between employers and employees when negotiations fail. ACAS offers several services:

- Preventing and resolving industrial disputes
- Resolving individual complaints regarding discrimination, unfair dismissal or employee rights
- Providing a source of information to business on employee issues, for example, reducing absenteeism and sickness levels

You also need to be aware of relevant legislation in this area. This includes:

- Trade Union Act 1984
- Trade Union Reform and Employment Rights Act 1993
- Working time Regulations 1998
- Race Relations Act 1976
- Disability and Discrimination Act 1994
- Equal Pay Act 1970
- Sex Discrimination Act 1974
- Employment Acts 1980,1982,1988, 1990
- Minimum Wage Act 1998
- Employment Relations Act 2000

Human resource management (HRM)

This is the process by which a business ensures that it makes the most efficient use of its employees. HRM can be either 'hard' or 'soft'.

- **Hard HRM** regards employees as a resource that needs to be allocated efficiently and effectively throughout its operation to achieve objectives.
- **Soft HRM** regards employees as being the most valuable asset to the business. Employees should be encouraged to develop and maximise their potential and value, thus helping the business to develop and reach its potential. This is a long-term strategy to achieve.

Workforce planning is a key activity of HRM. It considers the likely future employee needs of the company, taking into account organisational aims and objectives. It examines the current and projected supply of labour available in conjunction with the current and expected demands for labour in the future, whilst carrying out an internal skill audit to see what labour the company already possesses. In simple terms workforce planning is the identification of skills gaps (or over capacity) in the current and anticipated employee requirements, and the plans formulated to ensure the company has the right combination of employees available now and in the future. This could involve:

- Recruitment
- Training
- Redundancies
- Redeployment

Methods of remuneration

This was covered in *Do Brilliantly AS Business Studies*, Chapter 3.

Measurement of personnel effectiveness

Labour productivity is given by the formula:

$$\text{Labour productivity} = \frac{\text{Output per time period}}{\text{Number of employees}}$$

Labour turnover is given by the formula:

$$\text{Labour turnover} = \frac{\text{Number of staff leaving}}{\text{Average number of staff}} \times 100$$

Absenteeism is given by:

$$\text{Absenteeism} = \frac{\text{Number of staff absent that day}}{\text{Total number of staff}} \times 100$$

Health and safety is given by:

$$\text{Health and safety} = \frac{\text{Number of working days lost}}{\text{Total number of working days}} \times 100$$

Key points to remember

Operations management

Productive efficiency

Research and development is the creation of new products or process through the application of scientific research and technical development. R&D is expensive and time consuming and is only beneficial if developments can be turned into commercially viable products. It is especially important in fast-moving technological industries. Successful R&D leads to innovation and this allows firms to keep ahead of their competitors. However, few ideas ever make commercial success and so R&D is a substantial risk.

Critical path analysis is the analytical system for breaking a project into its components activities to allow for the scheduling of the most efficient sequence. It is a method of network analysis that aims to complete projects in the shortest timescale possible by examining which activities can be completed simultaneously.

Advantages
- Managers must consider all aspects of a project before it starts, increasing understanding and the coordination of resources and personnel.
- Shortens project development time though the identification of the quickest pathway.
- Identifies when projects should be completed. This is crucial, for example in developing a new product for launch, as retailers and advertisers will all need to know launch dates in advance.

Disadvantages
- Uses forecasted figures, which can give inaccurate or misleading information.
- CPA shows the quickest pathway to complete a project. It does not show whether the project is the best possible use of the firm's resources.
- CPA is only a network diagram – it does not ensure that projects are managed effectively or efficiently – although it can then be used for monitoring and review.

Controlling operations

Application of IT systems

You need to first review the AS aspects of this area. This was covered in *Do Brilliantly AS Business Studies*, Chapter 4.

IT can be used to generate a competitive advantage over rivals. Through the provision of increasingly accurate and up-to-date information, it can help managers assimilate and interpret data as well as communicate findings to others. This is a huge aid to decision making from market research to project implementation. Information Technology systems can also benefit a business through:
- **Improved stock control** – Automatic monitoring and re-order systems can prevent stock-outs and over-stocking and is a massive benefit to operating JIT stock control.
- **Cost saving** – Examination of supplier websites lead to quick and easy information on material costs, allowing companies to save time and money on purchasing decisions. It also provides for the use of remote teleworking, saving on office overheads and expenses.
- **CAD/CAM** – Computer-aided deign and computer-aided manufacturing can lead to more efficient, less wasteful methods of production. It also allows for faster design and development times.
- **Accounting systems** – Spreadsheets and databases can be used to construct automatic routines for recording financial information, thus allowing managers to access up-to-date reports on profits, cashflow and financial stability. This improves decisions and reduces the financial risk of making poor decisions at inappropriate times.

Building a business

Sandra came over from Portugal when she was just seventeen. Several years of cleaning jobs enabled her to build up some savings, but it was only when she met – and later married – Pablo that she stopped being haunted by poverty. Pablo was a chef, working in kitchens in South London and working very hard. Both were keen to start their own business and it seemed obvious to build it around Pablo's cooking skills. This vague thought gained focus after a dinner party at which Pablo cooked for eight English friends. All were openly impressed by the Portuguese food, with one saying: 'That's not only the best meal I've had in ages, it's also the most interesting. I find Chinese food and Indian pretty samey these days.'

Two of the friends asked if Pablo could produce the same meal for 30 guests at their son's wedding. This was done with great success and significant profit. Word of mouth spread further and soon Sandra and Pablo had a nice little business sideline. The business was able to achieve the known profit benchmark for the catering trade, a 300% mark-up. In other words a dish they could charge £4 for, cost £1 to make. With that in view, Pablo was convinced they could succeed. However, it became increasingly difficult to meet customer orders from their own small kitchen.

Shortly afterwards Sandra heard of a local restaurant that had closed. It had a large, newly equipped kitchen and good access for deliveries. It cost £10 000 to buy the lease plus £1000 per month to rent. The lease would use up half their savings but they were determined to proceed. Pablo had still not given up his regular job and salary, so Sandra was doing most of the cooking and organising. The strain was beginning to affect Sandra's health, so her young sister came over from Portugal for a few months to help out.

With her sister working in the kitchen, Sandra visited some local pubs to see if any of them would be interested in adding a special Portuguese section to their menu. Dishes such as 'Pork and Clams' and 'Salt Cod Chowder' were rejected out of hand by most, but after days of rejection, Sandra found one pub with a more adventurous customer base. At 11.30 a.m. every day Sandra would deliver the fully and freshly prepared food, in 400 gram portions, then the pub microwaved the food plus rice. It proved a huge hit and once again supply pressures became acute.

By July 1998 Pablo was at last able to resign from his job and work full-time for the business. On advice from their bank they incorporated Porto Foods Ltd, and hired a bright young accountant (Sonal) to work one day a week to provide some financial expertise. Within six months local trade was generating an annual equivalent of £300 000 turnover and £25 000 profit. Pablo was training and organising a food-preparation staff of eight part-time workers, while Sandra focused on getting and supplying customers.

Then came a call from J D Wetherspoons. This huge, national pub chain was interested in placing a regular order for Portuguese menu items that could be worth over £1.5 million in a full year. Rashly, Sandra agreed to a meeting in five days time. It soon became apparent that this was too short a time to think through the implications. Luckily, the accountant had been working on financial forecasts and an interim balance sheet, so some evidence existed.

It was difficult to calculate all the costs of producing and delivering so many meals to so many places. Pablo phoned round his catering trade contacts and received quick quotes on computer-aided machinery to produce and package most of the food automatically. This very expensive equipment could be rented, but at high monthly charges. Would it be worth it or would labour be more cost effective and more flexible?

Whatever else, accepting the order would make it necessary to move from the restaurant to a purpose-built factory unit. Large-scale industrial fridges, freezers and washing-up machines, plus conveyor-belt packing lines would be inevitable. It would also be essential to appoint experienced managers to handle delivery and administration. A series of meetings between Sonal, Pablo and Sandra led to the estimates shown in Appendices A and B. Two were spent on the balance sheet alone, with Sonal requiring a great deal of convincing of Pablo's logic: 'We can depreciate the equipment over a five-year not a three-year period. That will boost profit and strengthen the balance sheet as collateral for raising the extra loans we're going to need'. Sonal estimated that £120 000 would be required to finance the capital expenditure plus working capital requirements for the Wetherspoon's order. This would only be possible if the bank was very generous with loans, or if suppliers were very generous with credit terms.

Now they had to decide whether to accept the order or not.

Appendix A
(Sonal's estimates prior to discussion with Pablo)

Porto Foods Ltd Interim Balance Sheet (unaudited) Dec 31st 2001

Fixed Assets	£28 500
Stock	£2 500
Debtors and Cash	£18 000
Current Liabilities	(£7 000)
ASSETS EMPLOYED	£42 000
Loans	£12 000
Shareholder's funds	£30 000
CAPITAL EMPLOYED	£42 000

Appendix B

Porto Foods Ltd key data as at Jan 10th 2002

Current operations	Jan 2002	July 2001
% of customer complaints/returns	0.08%	0.12%
Stock turnover (times per year)	127.5	104.2
Productivity (portions per worker per hour)	15.5	11.8
Raw material stock wastage	8.4%	8.9%

Financial appraisal of renting new computerised machinery	
Impact on capacity	+100%
Impact on productivity	+35%

Appendix C

Current break-even data

Output	75 000 units
Fixed costs	£200 000
Variable cost (per unit)	£1.00
Selling price (per unit)	£4.00
Current BE output	66 667 units

1 (a) Would you consider Sandra and Pablo to have been asset-led in their approach to marketing their business? Explain your answer. [8 marks]

(b) In this early phase of their business, Sandra and Pablo seem to have made marketing decisions largely based on instinct. Consider whether they might have benefited from using the marketing model. [12 marks]

2 (a) Porto's development plan will push capacity up by 100%, increasing fixed costs to £350 000 while variable costs would fall to 80p per unit. Selling price would remain at £4.

    (i) Construct a break-even chart for the new position. [6 marks]

    (ii) Indicate and state the new break-even output. [2 marks]

(b) On the basis of the graph and the other **financial** information available, should Porto Foods accept the order? Justify your answer. [12 marks]

3 (a) Use the evidence in Appendix B to analyse the effectiveness of Porto personnel over the last six months. [10 marks]

(b) Discuss whether computer-aided manufacturing is an appropriate operations strategy for Porto Foods Ltd. [10 marks]

4 Assuming Porto Foods continues to expand, discuss the main problems Sandra and Pablo may face in handling the people **and** operations aspects of the business. [20 marks]

Examiner's hints
- In question 1 (b) it is not necessary to define the marketing model and its stages. The question requires a discussion as to whether its use would have benefited or not benefited Porto Foods Ltd.
- For question 2 (a) (ii), a handy hint is to work this out using formulae rather than trying to read off your chart.
- For question 3 (a) a good form of analysis is to look at proportional changes in figures, i.e. the degree of change not just the physical amount.
- Question 4 is asking you to consider **two** topic areas and to gain full marks you must discuss implications for **both** these subjects.

Answers can be found on pages 91–96.

Exam Question and Answer

Textico

Textico is a medium-sized manufacturer of shirts based in Lancashire, which at present sells only in the home market. It sells some of its shirts under its own name; others are sold under the retailer's own label name. It is facing increasingly strong competition from cheap imports. It has a full capacity output of 600 000 shirts per annum. However, current forecasts for 2002 predict sales of only 325 000 at £5 per shirt, well below the break-even level of 400 000. In an effort to improve its financial performance, the Sales Manager has negotiated two potential contracts. One is with an English retailer, Fashion Plus, which would sell the shirts under the retailer's own brand name. The other is with a German retailer, Schmidt, which would allow the Textico brand to be introduced to a new export market.

The Managing Director has requested you, as Sales Manager, to write a report, making a fully justified recommendation as to whether one or both of the contracts should be accepted.

[Total 40 marks, including 2 for an appropriate report format]

Appendices

APPENDIX A	Textico sales data: Number of shirts sold 1999–2001
APPENDIX B	Textico profit and loss account 2000–2002
APPENDIX C	Provisional details of proposed contacts for Textico
APPENDIX D	Schmidt and Fashion Plus: Sales growth and number of retail outlets 1999–2001
APPENDIX E	Economic forecasts for 2002–2004

Appendix A

Textico sales data: Number of shirts sold 1999–2001

Year	Textico brand sales	Retailers' own label sales		Total Sales
		Store A	Store B	
1999	400 000	70 000	25 000	**495 000**
2000	350 000	50 000	50 000	**450 000**
2001	300 000		60 000	**360 000**

Appendix B

Textico profit and loss account 2000–2002

	2000 (£)	2001 (£)	2002 (forecast*) (£)
Turnover	2 240 000	1 736 000	1 625 000
Cost of sales	850 000	781 000	731 250
Gross profit	1 390 000	955 000	893 750
Expenses	1 350 000	1 200 000	1 100 000
Net profit	40 000	-245 000	-206 250

* forecast excludes new contracts

Appendix C

Provisional details of proposed contacts for Textico

	Fashion Plus	Schmidt
Quantity	200 000	120 000
Delivery	over next 12 months	over next 6 months
Price per shirt	£4.00	€6.75
Contribution per shirt	£1.75	£2.25*
Total contribution	£350 000	£270 000
Credit terms	90 days	60 days

* Assuming current exchange rate: £1 = €1.5 (where € = Euro)

Appendix D

Schmidt and Fashion Plus: Sales growth and number of retail outlets 1999–2001

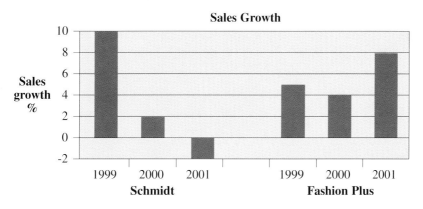

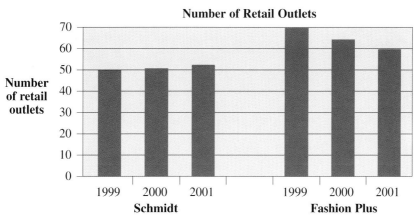

Appendix E

Economic forecasts for 2002–2004 (Average annual percentage changes)

	UK (%)	Germany (%)
Economic growth	2.5	2.00
Consumer spending in real terms	2.00	1.50
Retail clothes price index	-2.00	1.00

FABIAN'S ANSWER

A REPORT CONSIDERING TWO POSSIBLE CONTRACTS

From: Fabian Deveraux, Sales Manager
To: The Managing Director (Textico)

TERMS OF REFERENCE

To analyse critically the information on two different contracts (Schmidt and Fashion Plus) and make a fully justified recommendation which one (or both) should be accepted.

PROCEDURE

I will examine each of the appendices and consider the strengths and weaknesses of each possibility and then use this information to come to a decision about which one I would recommend to the Managing Director.

FINDINGS

APPENDIX A

Weaknesses
This appendix shows a big weakness as it gives Textico's total sales data and from this it can be seen that Textico's total sales have fallen over the last two years from 495 000 to 360 000. This is quite a large fall and would appear to be because Store A has stopped selling own label shirts completely. Another weakness is that Textico's own brand sales have dropped as well (400 000 to 300 000).

Strengths
Store B is doing quite well as its sales of shirts have increased.

The problem for Textico is that, as it says in the case study, they need 400 000 shirts to break-even but they only actually sell 360 000 in total.

APPENDIX B

Weaknesses
This appendix shows Textico's profit and loss account and again reveals quite a large problem for the company. The main area of concern is that the company is now making a loss (2001 figures) and is forecast to make an even bigger one in the future, although this does exclude the possible contracts. The accounts also show falling turnover figures which decrease even more on the forecast account.

Strengths
The only strength from this appendix is that their costs are falling as well. As you can see, expenses have gone down from 1 350 000 to 1 100 000, although this is

perhaps to be expected as they are making less, so it should really cost them less.

This appendix would indicate that the company definitely needs to accept one or both of the contracts or they will eventually become bankrupt and be forced to close down.

For this appendix I am going to consider each contract in turn.

Fashion Plus

This looks quite good for the company. It is a big contract of 200 000 shirts which would make the company break even and put them close to full capacity – 560 000 shirts altogether out of a possible 600 000 over the next year. It also makes a total contribution for the company of £350 000 which is more than the Schmidt contract makes (although this is only for six months). The weakness of this contract is that Fashion Plus want 90 days credit terms. This means it would be effectively three months before Textico got paid and this could cause them to experience some cashflow problems.

Schmidt

This contract is only half as long as the one with Fashion Plus – it only lasts six months. However, because of the 60 day credit terms Textico would get their money a lot sooner than with the first one. The problem is that this contract does not make as much money for them – only £270 000. There is another possible problem (although this could be an advantage as well) – it assumes that exchange rates stay stable. If this isn't the case, then Textico may receive less money than they thought. Alternatively, though they could get more if the exchange rate improves.

This information would suggest that Fashion Plus is the better contract as it makes the company more money in total and would not be at risk from fluctuating exchange rates.

APPENDIX D

For this appendix I am again going to consider each contract.

Fashion Plus

From graph 1 we can see that Fashion Plus' sales are growing by up to 8% per year. This is good news as it means they will need more shirts to sell in future. However, from graph 2 it looks like Fashion Plus have fewer shops each year. If this continues then the company may not want more shirts.

Schmidt

Schmidt is the other way round from Fashion Plus. From graph 2 we can see that Schmidt actually have more shops each year, but their sales growth is declining. This again means that they may want more or less shirts in future depending on what happens. Perhaps as Schmidt want to sell the Textico brand in Germany they are looking for new fashions to boost their falling sales. This could be quite good as it would mean they might place lots of orders, which would benefit Textico.

From this information it is difficult to determine exactly which one is the better as they both could go either way.

APPENDIX E

I am going to examine this information country by country as Fashion Plus is based in England and Schmidt is in Germany so it is best to do it like this.

UK

There are some parts of this that again look quite encouraging. Economic growth is forecast to be 2.5% which is quite good, because as the economy grows more people have jobs so they spend more. This can be seen in the fact that consumer spending is also forecast to rise by 2.00%. Altogether this probably means that more people with more money will buy more clothes, particularly fashion items that are considered to be luxury goods and which are therefore responsive to consumers' incomes. In this case then, we can assume that perhaps people in the UK will buy more shirts. One negative point is that the retail price index has fallen by -2.00%.

Germany

Germany's economic information is fairly similar to the UK's in that growth and spending are again going up. Again this means that people in Germany may buy more shirts. However, these figures are going up less than in the UK. The appendix says that:

	UK	Germany
Economic growth	2.5%	2.00%
Consumer spending	2.00%	1.50%

which shows that probably the UK is better.

The retail price index isn't falling, as it is in the UK. This perhaps means that there is inflation in Germany so maybe people won't buy as much.

This information would again suggest to me that Fashion Plus is the best contract as it appears the UK is growing more than Germany.

RECOMMENDATIONS AND CONCLUSION

Considering all the information given, I would personally recommend that the company accepts the Fashion Plus contract. They definitely need to do something as they are not even breaking even at the moment and are making a loss. The Fashion Plus contract lasts for a whole year, which provides the company with more guaranteed work than Schmidt's would. It also makes more money in total and there is no risk of exchange rate fluctuations. Fashion Plus' sales are growing. Although they have fewer shops, the shops they have got are doing really well and the UK's economy is set to grow in future. All this information means that I would choose the Fashion Plus contract instead of Schmidt's.

21/40

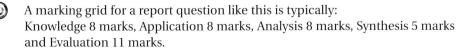

How to score full marks

- A marking grid for a report question like this is typically:
  Knowledge 8 marks, Application 8 marks, Analysis 8 marks, Synthesis 5 marks and Evaluation 11 marks.
  Emphasis is given to the skill of evaluation. **Synthesis is a new skill that only appears on the marking grid for the report**. As we analyse Fabian's answer, pay particular attention to the way in which links could have been developed.
  Marks awarded to Fabian's answer: Knowledge 5 (including 2 for report format), Application 4, Analysis 3, Synthesis 3 and Evaluation 6. Total 21.

- When answering the report question, **your style of answering is a key to success**. Fabian has used a common approach to this question by deciding that he is going to look at each appendix in turn and decide strengths and weaknesses. This is a reasonable idea but, as you can see, as Fabian progresses through the report his approach breaks down and he has to change the format with which he approaches each section. **This does not help Fabian present a coherent and connected report format**. This style of response also makes it difficult to attain good marks for **analysis** and **synthesis**.

- **A better approach is to consider the merits and demerits of each proposition, given Textico's circumstances**. This allows you to draw together and **link information** from the various appendices relating to each possibility. By doing this, **you achieve a much greater degree of analysis as you present your argument for each contract as a connected whole**. Similarly, this helps achieve full marks for synthesis as you present a structure to the examiner that is consistent and easy to follow.

- Fabian makes a good start to this question by using an appropriate report format. This gains him the first marks for knowledge. However, his analysis of Appendix A is very weak. Fabian will gain low-level knowledge marks for explaining the data and some marks for application as he relates his approach slightly to Textico's break-even position. **He has not, though, related his analysis to the possible contract choices at all.** Fabian could have analysed the fact that Schmidt contract requires Textico brand shirts, whereas Fashion Plus want their own label to be manufactured. The appendix shows Textico brand sales to be far greater than own label, although declining. As a strategy for the company it is perhaps better to try and expand and promote its own brand name rather than the retailer's own.

This can also be linked to Appendix C where contribution per unit is higher for Schmidt's order than Fashion Plus's. A sensible conclusion from this link is that the selling price of a branded product is likely to be higher than that of a retailer's own label good. A final point on Appendix A is that Fabian states '*Store A has stopped selling own label shirts completely*'. This is probably incorrect; it is more likely that Textico has lost the contract and that Store A is selling own label shirts manufactured for them by someone else. The key point here is that it is also far easier to lose own-label contracts to competitors than contracts for branded goods. Competitors could not produce these, as they would be protected by copyright and trademarks, thus perhaps the Schmidt order provides greater security.

With Appendix B, **Fabian merely explains some of the data given, again only achieving low order marks.** He has failed to mention the way in which this information affects the decision that has to be made, i.e. choose Fashion Plus, Schmidt, or both? **This is an excellent opportunity for some good analysis to be made through the use of financial ratios**. This would have revealed the fact that as well as declining sales and profits, one of Textico's main problems is the level of expenses that get proportionately higher each year. This indicates a fall in the efficiency of the organisation as a whole and something that needs to be solved, quite apart from which order is accepted. **Pointing this out would help to achieve full marks for evaluation as it shows that you are aware of a range of issues that the firm actually needs to tackle, not just the simple scenario given of which contract to accept.**

The information in Appendix B can also be used to determine the company's current level of average contribution from existing customers, i.e. for 2001 the company has total sales of 360 000 and a gross profit of £955 000, giving an average contribution per shirt of £2.65. **This again can be linked with Appendix C,** where it can be seen that Textico would need spare capacity of 320 000 units to be able to fulfil both orders (when it only possesses 600 000 – 360 000 = 240 000 units). The higher contribution from existing customers over either possible contract suggests immediately that Textico must only accept one option, as it would lose money if it were to replace existing customers. **This line of approach would provide good marks for analysis, application and synthesis as it helps to provide an appropriate conclusion that relates directly to Textico's circumstances,** i.e. in its present state it cannot accept both contracts – one of the options presented in the case study.

When considering Appendix C, the structure of Fabian's answer improves because he has started **to compare each option and relate the information in the appendix to how Textico might be affected**. He has considered the payments terms, for example, and cashflow problems, although this area could have been discussed with more depth and analysis. He has also considered the risks associated with fluctuating exchange rates as well as a brief discussion regarding the level of contribution made, capacity and break-even.

This appendix provides many opportunities for some good links and analysis to be made. Possible lines of development include:

- Link to Appendix A, and discussion of the likelihood of repeat orders with Schmidt requiring branded products and therefore the implication that Schmidt actually becomes far more profitable over a 12-month basis than Fashion Plus. Or alternatively, that the information on Store B shows a potential for tremendous growth in the own label area.

- Link to Appendix D, and a discussion of the relative size and prospects of each of the potential customers. Again this affects the chances of repeat orders and the level of risk associated with each.

A good aspect of Fabian's approach to this appendix, though, is that **he summarises at the end how this information may affect his eventual conclusion. This helps direct the examiner along Fabian's line of reasoning.**

With Appendix D, his response again becomes slightly weak. Fabian has provided a basic discussion of the figures and limited development of the possible implications, but his approach is lacking in depth and insight. He would have done well to discuss the level of risk and costs associated with overseas and domestic sales respectively, as well as the degree of experience held by the company in each area and the level of difficulty in establishing a UK brand name in a foreign country.

Appendix D should ideally be linked with Appendix E to allow you to make reasoned judgements on the likely future sales growth in each country, again helping to establish which of the contracts may be the better option. Fabian has actually discussed this area quite well in his response to Appendix E. **However, he has not drawn the two aspects together**, which would be the ideal way to achieve full marks for analysis and synthesis. A major criticism here is that Fabian has actually copied out the figures provided in Appendix E – this gains no marks and just wastes time.

Fabian does also appear slightly confused about the meaning and implications of the retail price index information. A good line of argument here would have been to point out that a negative figure indicates falling prices and vice versa and the likely knock-on effects this might have for either contract – in terms of profitability (or contribution made) and the effect on demand and the prospect of repeat orders. This line of reasoning could have been linked to information in Appendices A, B, C respectively, again helping to reach a fully reasoned and justified conclusion.

Fabian's conclusion is excellent. **He has reached a definite recommendation, which is what the question asks for**. Frequently candidates conclude the report by stating that they cannot reach a decision as they would like more information. This approach would only achieve low level evaluation marks and is a technique that you should avoid. Fabian's conclusion is also a summary of all his main arguments why Fashion Plus is the best choice. This focuses the examiner on his logic and reasoning throughout his response and draws his argument together. This helps to gain marks for synthesis.

In summary, Fabian's response has shown some knowledge and limited development of several points. He has at times applied the information to the scenario and the decision to be made and reached a definite and reasoned conclusion. **However, he has not linked any appendices together and he did not follow a coherent and consistent approach. The analysis presented was lacking in depth and insight and although he wrote a conclusion, he missed several key points in his response.** This explains why he only achieved half the possible marks available.

To gain full marks you would have needed to explore some of the **links** demonstrated above. You would need to **focus your reasoning at all times on how the evidence affects the decision to made.** To achieve full marks for evaluation, you need to not only analyse the information, but also **judge its relative importance,** i.e. what are the key issues facing the firm? An example of this is the necessity for Textico to control its costs in relation to its sales (see Appendix B), not just to gain more sales. High marks for evaluation are also gained by candidates who are able to **present a comprehensive solution**. In this case, you could have raised the possibility that the firm should accept both contracts, but that this would only be possible if Textico hired temporary workers, leased extra machinery on short-term leases and subcontracted basic operations to provide increased capacity. This would then allow them to see if Schmidt and/or Fashion Plus would become regular or one-off customers at little risk to themselves.

If you feel that a line of reasoning is relevant to more than one appendix, don't be afraid to use it twice. **Often the inter-linkages between business variables mean that similar effects will become apparent from entirely different causes.**

Don't copy out material from the appendices as this does not demonstrate any skills being examined and gains no marks.

To get top-level marks on many case study questions, it is necessary to relate your answers to the context of the business and the scenario given. **Think about how situations would affect the individual business you are given.**

The information in the case study is there to help you. Not all of it will be equally relevant. However, **you must consider some aspect of each appendix to achieve full marks.**

Good analysis often involves looking at figures proportionately, i.e. a rise in net profit from 8% to 10% is actually a 25% increase.

Make sure you **read the case study data carefully**. A good technique is to skim it quickly once to get the general idea. Then re-read it **carefully highlighting important points and forming links between appendices.**

Know how to present a report and how to construct your answer. By following a coherent and consistent structure your marks will improve.

The case study is a numerate application. **Make sure you have all the equipment necessary such as a calculator.**

Evaluation relies on reaching a reasoned definite judgement, stemming from the arguments given in your answer. Evaluation that relies on statements or assertion that something is so, will gain few if any marks.

Report format

The format of the report should include:
- **Title**
- **From**: *Your name and position*
- **To**: *Their name and position*
- **Date**: *dd/mm/yy*

The body of the report should then be subdivided into clear sections, with each section clearly headed.
- The arguments for option A
- The arguments against option A
- The arguments for option B
- The arguments against option B

The details of each section should contain clearly developed points that link information from the appendices and relate directly to the decision to be made. Each appendix should be considered at least once in the body of your response.

- **Conclusion and recommendations**
  This should contain a definite recommendation with a summary that draws together the key points that have influenced you in making your decision.

  Note: It is not necessary to include terms of reference, procedures or an introduction.

Do ...

... look for links between the appendices – this provides good lines of developed analysis.

... make a definite recommendation. **There is no single correct answer.** As long as you justify why you've chosen your option you can achieve full marks.

... consider the realistic options available to the business. Look at its size, strengths, resources and experience, then you can make a recommendation the business can fulfil.

... use a formal report format. This is the best way of keeping your answers coherent and focused.

Don't ...

... try to write about all the information. This will take too long – be selective and analyse only the most important aspects.

... take too much time. The essay questions in section two for AQA candidates are worth the same amount of marks.

... trot through the appendices one by one as Fabian did. Consider each option in turn as a connected whole.

... over-calculate. The use of financial ratios or other formulae may prove useful at times. However, the focus of the question is on reaching a justified recommendation for future action, not just assessing its current position.

Cityspeed

Cityspeed operates bus services in the small city of Traverton. As part of its forward planning, Cityspeed needs to choose between two investment projects, either purchasing new vehicles or building a new depot, as it does not have sufficient finance to fund both schemes.

It has one local competitor, Destina, which has recently put in service some of the latest low-floor, easy-access buses. These vehicles make travel easier, particularly for elderly people and mothers with young children. Cityspeed is considering whether it should order 15 similar new vehicles. In addition, it has received an offer from a developer for its present city centre operating base. This provides Cityspeed with an opportunity to build a new, purpose-built depot with improved maintenance facilities on an industrial estate two miles from the city centre.

As Cityspeed's financial adviser, you are required to produce a report for the Board of Directors assessing the two proposed investments and recommending which one should be adopted.

[Total 40 marks, including 2 marks for an appropriate report format]

Appendices

APPENDIX A   Benchmarking data for operations of Cityspeed and Destina
APPENDIX B   Cityspeed maintenance report
APPENDIX C   Traverton population trends
APPENDIX D   Investment appraisal statistics for Cityspeed's proposals
APPENDIX E   Financial ratios based on Cityspeed's accounts for 1999 and 2000

Appendix A

Benchmarking data for operations of Cityspeed and Destina

	Cityspeed	Destina
Current bus fleet size	70	50
Average age of fleet	10 years	5 years
No. low-floor buses	0	10
Passenger journeys 1998	5.0m	3.0m
Passenger journeys 2000	4.5m	4.2m
Fare revenue per passenger mile 1998	16p	15p
Fare revenue per passenger mile 2000	16p	18p
Net profit 1998	£0.7m	£0.2m
Net profit 2000	£0.5m	£0.3m

Appendix B

Cityspeed maintenance record

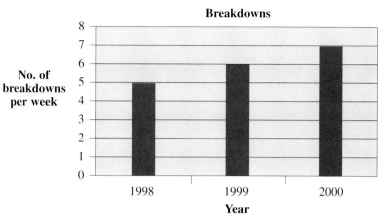

Breakdowns

No. of breakdowns per week

Maintenance Cost

Maintenance cost per vehicle per annum (£)

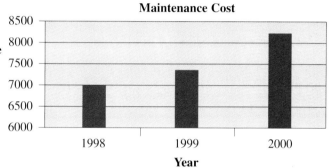

Appendix C

Traverton population trends

	1991	2001	2011(FORECAST)
Total population	210 000	230 000	240 000
Of which: aged over 60	42 000	48 000	55 000
aged under 11	24 000	22 000	20 000

Appendix D

Investment appraisal statistics for Cityspeed's proposals

	New vehicles	New depot
Initial outlay	£1.5m	£1.0m*
Expected life	15 years	30 years
Payback	6 years	5 years
Average rate of return	10%	8%
Net present value at 6% discount rate	£850 000	£700 000

* assuming £2m is received from the sale of the old depot

Appendix E

Financial ratios based on Cityspeed's accounts for 1999 and 2000

Year	1999	2000
Gearing	44%	40%
Acid test	0.7	0.7
Return on capital	11.10%	10.30%

Examiner's hints

- Consider the information contained in each appendix and try to **make reasoned links between them**. For example, Appendix D and E both obviously relate to financial information. However, so does Appendix A, in part.
- **Look at the company's strengths and weaknesses as well as the opportunities and threats**. You do not need to conduct a SWOT analysis, but this is nevertheless a good basis to construct your arguments around.
- Remember that in the scenario, you have been hired as a financial advisor to recommend **which** of the two options should be adopted. **This means you must reach an absolute conclusion as to which option is best and why.** Full marks for evaluation are awarded for appropriate conclusions justified by the evidence, showing an awareness of the most relevant underlying themes or issues and their potential implications.

Answers can be found on pages 96–97.

4 Essay Questions

1 'Convention dictates that a company looks after its shareholders first, its customers next and last of all worries about its employees. Virgin does the opposite.' *Richard Branson.* Evaluate how adopting this approach of putting employees rather than shareholders first might affect the performance of a business. [40 marks]

2 Several industries, for example gas and electricity, have been forced by the government to reduce prices and allow more competition. To what extent might such government intervention be desirable for businesses and their consumers? [40 marks]

3 Many major take-overs and mergers involve substantial job losses. Does this mean that these mergers and take-overs are bad for British business? [40 marks]

4 In 2000, both Ford and Vauxhall (General Motors) announced plans to end car production at one of their British car factories. To what extent might these closure decisions be the result of the high value of the pound? [40 marks]

Note: In the actual AQA paper 5W, candidates must choose one from the above four. To help with exam technique, we will consider responses to all four essays.

---

1 Convention dictates that a company looks after its shareholders first, its customers next and last of all worries about its employees. Virgin does the opposite.' *Richard Branson.* Evaluate how adopting this approach of putting employees rather than shareholders first might affect the performance of a business. [40 marks]

INDIA'S ANSWER

The key to this question is how might this affect the performance of a business. In reality there are two aspects to this. Firstly, how might performance be enhanced and secondly, in what ways could the actual performance deteriorate?

First, by concentrating on its employees, the business is going to benefit in several ways. By putting its workforce before all other stakeholders the company is doing its best to ensure that they will have a motivated workforce. The workforce should feel valued, wanted and important. In line with the studies produced by Elton Mayo and theories such as Maslow's hierarchy of needs, this will help meet some of the workforce's higher order needs. It will make them feel they are a valuable asset to the business and that their opinions and efforts are recognised and respected. This should improve business performance as motivated workers take less time off work (sickness and absenteeism), which reduces the costs of overtime or employing temporary staff and reduces lost production. Performance is enhanced as reduced costs naturally lead to greater profits.

With less lost productivity, the workers are, by definition, more productive. They also tend to be more productive if they are happy in their work as they try harder. With greater levels of production come economies of scale and again greater profits as the unit cost falls when fixed costs become spread across a larger output.

Thus, in these instances, performance has been increased in terms of reduced costs, greater output and higher profits.

Performance may also be enhanced because management are prepared to listen and act upon employees' concerns and their ideas. This greatly enhances the degree of communication between workforce and management and thus raises the degree of participation. From this stems the idea that the company, as a whole, may develop much better working practices and products as they listen to and implement the ideas of their employees.

With better working practices, performance will improve as efficiency increases: less mistakes are made, better quality products are produced and perhaps there is less duplication of effort and misallocation of resources. Better products of increased quality will attract more customers, so hopefully improving market share, sales levels and again profits. Thus it can be seen that putting your workforce first can enhance many areas of business performance.

However, all the above needs to be contrasted with the cost to the business that this incurs. Concentrating on workers' needs and putting them first could mean vast expenses on salary increases, bonuses and incentives. There might also need to be improved working conditions such as better environments, less hours and longer holidays. In these cases the lost time may far outweigh any productive benefits gained from motivated workers. Similarly, the greater expense could also outweigh any increases in sales or cost savings to be made. Thus overall, the workers may well be motivated and happy (when they are there) but the actual level of performance in financial terms would decrease.

I guess this question really comes down to what exactly is meant by the performance of the business. Is it financial or is it productivity per hour, for example? One could decrease whilst the other improves. In this instance, I would judge that Virgin might have got it right. Richard Branson seems to be able to run numerous successful branches of Virgin products using this approach and make large amounts of profit into the bargain. Perhaps this approach wouldn't be suitable for every business like smaller companies, for example. But as stated, in this instance it seems to work and work quite well.

28/40

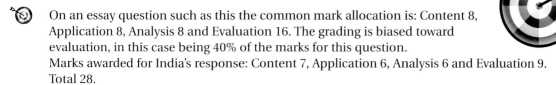

How to score full marks

On an essay question such as this the common mark allocation is: Content 8, Application 8, Analysis 8 and Evaluation 16. The grading is biased toward evaluation, in this case being 40% of the marks for this question.
Marks awarded for India's response: Content 7, Application 6, Analysis 6 and Evaluation 9. Total 28.

The first impression of India's answer is that it has depth, is well written and puts forward a balanced argument. However, this is not strictly the case when you consider the actual question. **India has provided an excellent response on the benefits and costs of putting the workforce first but has not included any discussion or consideration of shareholders and customers.**

India's style of writing and the way in which she presents her arguments are very good. She is **using clearly defined paragraphs for each point and develops each argument through several well-constructed and connected points.** The first paragraph is really an introduction and doesn't merit any marks. Nevertheless, it is quite brief, so she hasn't wasted too much time, and does set the scene nicely.

In paragraphs two and three, India gives a good presentation of arguments that would support Richard Branson's approach, with the inclusion of **relevant theorists and a linked discussion of exactly how and what benefits may occur.** The really good point about these is the way in which India has focused her answer on how the performance of the business is affected, i.e. **she has identified the trigger and applied her answer to it.**

India has continued this line through paragraphs three and four and again **taken her points through a series of in-depth analyses.** A criticism here would be that up to this point India has written rather a lot and actually developed four points where perhaps two or three would be sufficient. So, **she has penalised herself in terms of time** and this becomes more apparent with the rather brief (in comparison) consideration of the other side of the argument later on.

Paragraph five does consider some of the drawbacks, but this is where her answer perhaps loses focus. Really she should be considering the advantages of putting shareholders or customers first as the question directs. So while she is gaining some marks for her analytical skills, she is unable to achieve full marks as she has gone off the point.

Her final evaluative paragraph is excellent given her argument, **but again is not wholly focused on the trade off between employee's and shareholder's needs**. This question really was about stakeholder analysis and India has missed this. Good points though include her discussion of what performance is, although she does not reach a clear judgement. For example, in most companies, particularly those with shareholders, profit performance is perhaps the key measure. She does provide some judgement concerning the relative merits and success of this strategy, but it is a rather sweeping and general statement – not all of Virgin's enterprises are as successful as others. Similarly, she fails to develop why it might not be suitable for a smaller business (e.g. lack of resources).

India's answer would have been enhanced by a discussion of shareholders and perhaps customers, and an evaluation considering the long- and short-term implications. For example, the sacrifice of short-term profits to improve employee motivation and performance should bring long-term increased profits for shareholders. However, in consumer-orientated industries such as the ones Virgin operates in, the customer should perhaps be put first.

2   Several industries, for example gas and electricity, have been forced by the government to reduce prices and allow more competition. To what extent might such government intervention be desirable for businesses and their consumers?   [40 marks]

PATRICK'S ANSWER

The deregulation and privatisation of British industries has been a common theme in UK government since the Thatcher years of the 1980s. This was designed to try and make the then state-owned and -run nationalised industries more efficient and more competitive. Basically, they were subsidised a lot by the government and the idea was that rather than being owned and run by the government on behalf of the people, if they became commercial enterprises then they would no longer be a drain on national resources. As profit-making companies they should, in fact, start paying money into the Treasury instead.

Actually, the government has benefited in several ways from this. First, the nationalised industries were sold off to the public by floating on the Stock Exchange and selling shares. This enabled the government to raise substantial amounts of money. In fact when you consider that they sold not only the electricity and gas but also water, trains and British Telecom, then the input into the government's funds would have been vast. So from this the government would seem to have benefited in many ways. However, as part of the process towards becoming commercially viable operations, the privatised industries actually laid off thousands of workers, so creating unemployment and decreasing income tax revenues as well as increasing the level of transfer payments such as dole money to the now unemployed.

One of the benefits to the businesses of reducing the workforce was that as they became leaner and fitter, business costs were reduced and they were able to enjoy larger profits. They were able to pass on cheaper prices to the consumer and it does say in the question that the businesses were forced to lower prices for customers.

Whether or not this has actually been a successful policy is perhaps a matter of some debate — the current state of UK railways and BT being examples. The railways may be cheaper (according to the question) but I don't believe they are. I live in Chelmsford and have often caught the train to London and my experience is that it is not cheaper unless you get a special deal and these are often inconvenient. Similarly, there are regular news stories about water companies and these never seem to be good news either.

However, it does seem that the electricity and gas companies have achieved some success. In these two areas, competition does appear to have flourished as per the government's intentions and the various companies are now all offering each others' services and claim to be cheaper than the next. I imagine (though I don't have exact information) that with all these companies competing for your business, prices must have fallen and therefore this is a definite benefit to consumers as they pay less.

So, has it been desirable or not? Well, the answer depends upon which privatised company you look at.

(9/40)

On an essay question such as this the common mark allocation is: Content 8, Application 8, Analysis 8 and Evaluation 16.
Marks awarded for Patrick's response: Content 3, Application 3, Analysis 2 and Evaluation 1. Total 9.

This is a classic example of a student whose answer has failed to focus on the question.

Paragraph one is a history lesson and has no Business Studies content at all. As an introduction all it manages to achieve is to waste time, a valuable resource in an exam.

Paragraph two then starts to offer some development. However, Patrick is considering the effect on the government not on businesses or consumers. The trigger for this question is **how (or not) government intervention** could be deemed to be **'desirable'** from the perspective of **'businesses'** and **'consumers'**. It is unlikely that a Business Studies question will have effects on government as its main focus.

It is only when we get half way through the third paragraph that the answer actually focuses on the question. Here there is a marginally developed point about saving costs.

The next paragraph really offers no development whatsoever. **The use of specific business examples is a good way of demonstrating application and analysis** in many cases, but in this example Patrick has offered anecdotal evidence only, i.e. no clear discussion of facts or case studies that would support his arguments.

Fortunately, in paragraph five Patrick does offer a little more content by outlining a benefit to consumers, but this is very limited in scope and depth. Here his arguments should have centred on benefits, such as reduced prices, contrasted with perhaps undesirable implications, such as drops in product quality or service levels, as companies cut costs to maintain profit levels.

Patrick's final evaluative sentence is really a statement. It does come in some part from his arguments, but as he has not addressed the question properly it is obvious that he has found evaluation difficult. If he had focused on the trigger words given, he would have found this a much easier task.

As with many Business Studies questions there is no right answer but you must answer the question! Some people are in favour of interventionist policies and the regulation of natural monopolies to prevent them abusing market power. Others, on the other hand, would argue for a more *laissez faire* approach and the free operation of market forces. Perhaps, with the specific nature of the products given as examples in this question, a stronger case could be made for intervention as gas and electricity could both be considered essential goods.

3 Many major take-overs and mergers involve substantial job losses. Does this mean that these mergers and take-overs are bad for British business? [40 marks]

RACHEL'S ANSWER

My first impression is to disagree with this statement, although I will consider both sides of the argument.

When a takeover or merger takes place it can be either a horizontal or vertical takeover, as well as being either a friendly or hostile manoeuvre such as a dawn raid on the Stock Exchange. A vertical takeover is one when a company takes over another company either above or below it in the supply chain. For example, a manufacturer takes over a chain of retailers, so it can now have its own shops to sell its product in, or purchases its own raw material suppliers so it no longer has to deal with an outside supplier. In both these cases, this cuts down the number of individual firms in the supply chain and thus the number of companies adding on their own small profit margins. This means, for example, that if a manufacturer did buy a supplier and a retailer, then instead of three sets of profit being added on, the one company now just adds on its profit once, and can add on more than it did as just one cog in the wheel. Therefore, the company can experience larger profit margins and the consumers get the same goods at cheaper prices, as the retailer now no longer adds on their bit of profit as well.

The business benefits in several ways. By taking over another company they are now bound to be bigger than they were, even if there are a few job losses, so they will benefit more from economies of scale, creating even better costs savings and profit margins than before. Coupled to this will be the effect that with lower prices there will be an increase in demand for the company's goods and services. This again increases output and sales leading to even greater economies being made. The company does have to be careful, though, as if it grows too large then diseconomies of scale will set in and the company will start to make a loss.

Alternatively, it could be a horizontal takeover, where a company takes over a business in the same sector and industry as itself. Thus essentially doing the same thing but just getting bigger. A good example of this might be when Granada took over the Forte Group, thus creating one large company doing the same thing. In this instance, cost savings can again be made through economies of scale such as purchasing economies — the company can benefit from discounts from bulk buying. Once more this could result in lower prices for the customer as the company becomes more competitive and passes these savings on.

But this is not always the case, with the merger of Lloyds and TSB for example, there were substantial job losses and branch closures as well. This meant that not only were people made unemployed but the customers did not benefit either as they perhaps lost access to their local branch and maybe staff with whom they were familiar as well. As the Bank of England sets interest rates, then really customers gained no price savings either. In fact just about the only people who would have benefited from this would have been the shareholders of the new company, as they would receive the extra profits made.

Focusing on the question though, this is not necessarily bad for British businesses. In each point I've raised so far, the business becomes better off. Different stakeholders gain or lose — some people lose jobs — however the ones who are left become more secure as they now work for a larger company. Customers could either gain or lose depending if cost savings are passed on in lower prices. Shareholders should gain from increased profits and hence dividends. The main point is that the business gains. By becoming larger it has more resources and more customers and so consequently lessens its level of risk. By being more profitable it will attract more investors and also have more profits for investment in machinery, training or R&D for example, thus becoming more competitive in the long run.

The main concern really is that if a company grows too large it may encounter diseconomies of scale, such as problems of communication and co-ordination, thus decreasing its operational efficiency and causing a decline in profitability. The larger company may be more profitable overall, but just not quite as efficient at generating it. Alternatively, I suppose one aspect that wouldn't be considered good for British businesses is if it were a foreign company taking over a British one. This happened with my local water company, which is now French. In this case, not only would there be job losses and increased unemployment, but also the government would not gain revenue, as all profits would flow overseas. This would then have a downward multiplier effect on the British economy. I'm not saying there would be a recession but it would not be good news. Also, the security of workers would not be any good because if the French company were to shut anywhere first, it would be the British subsidiary rather than their own domestic branch first. So in this case it definitely isn't good for British business.

To evaluate, I guess really the answer is that it depends on each individual circumstance. Some mergers and takeovers will prove beneficial to most stakeholder groups (except those made redundant) whereas some would prove to be a disadvantage to virtually all British stakeholders — it depends on the nature of the takeover and what the company does afterward. In reality, most mergers or take-overs probably must be regarded as being beneficial, as the Competition Commission vets them all and either says they're in the public interest or not and so determines if they can go ahead. For example, Lloyds TSB was allowed to proceed but the takeover of Manchester United by Sky was not.

 40/40

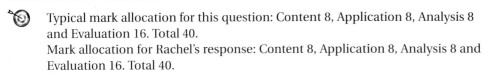

How to score full marks

- Typical mark allocation for this question: Content 8, Application 8, Analysis 8 and Evaluation 16. Total 40.
  Mark allocation for Rachel's response: Content 8, Application 8, Analysis 8 and Evaluation 16. Total 40.

- This is an excellent answer. It is not perfect – it does not consider every possible point, nor does it examine every point made in exhaustive detail. However, this is a good demonstration that **your answer does not have to be perfect to score full marks – it just has to be good enough.**

- **Rachel uses paragraphs to separate and delineate each point and skill being shown.** Each paragraph considers a separate point, explains why she considers it to be a benefit or a drawback and analyses why she thinks this is so. There are sound pieces of **evaluation made in the arguments** themselves, e.g. consideration of who benefits under differing circumstances, or the effect of the downward multiplier.

- Rachel's answer is an excellent example of how to **include real-life business examples to support your arguments**. This helps her to develop her points, gaining good marks for analysis as well as application.

- **The final evaluative paragraph** is an excellent example of good exam technique as well. Rachel does say, 'well it depends' which is perfectly correct, but she then goes on to state and explain exactly what factors it depends on, thus achieving evaluation marks by showing good judgement in determining relevant factors. The closing sentences regarding the operations of the Competition Commission are superb as they provide an indisputable line of reasoning for her final judgement and show an awareness of wider issues.

---

4 In 2000, both Ford and Vauxhall (General Motors) announced plans to end car production at one of their British car factories. To what extent might these closure decisions be the result of the high value of the pound? [40 marks]

MARK'S ANSWER

I think that this is highly likely as there have been constant stories in the press recently about how high our interest rates are compared with the rest of the world; the higher our rate of interest is then the stronger the pound becomes. This is because it becomes more attractive for foreign investors to save their money in the UK and to do so they need pounds so foreigners purchase our currency. As there is more demand for the pound and less of it around as more people are saving it, then correspondingly it becomes more expensive, i.e. the rate of exchange increases. This effectively increases the price of the pound in relation to other countries, therefore foreigners need more of their money to purchase one pound and the effect this has is to make goods made in the UK more expensive to them.

If, as in the case outlined, this happens then the more expensive a product is, the less demand there is for it and therefore the fewer goods the company sells. If a car company is selling fewer cars then obviously they don't need to make as many. As it is cars from the UK that are more expensive because of the high pound then it really does make sense to shut these factories rather than ones in other countries. So, in reality, the decision to shut the factories would relate directly to the high value of the pound.

In fact, I can't really see any way in which the high value of the pound could have helped these companies. No matter what, if the value of the pound is high then exports will be more expensive and therefore they will sell less as already stated. Imports will become cheaper as well but this doesn't help, as they need to export cars so really this has no effect.

In conclusion, I would have to agree with the statement that these closures are to do with the high value of the pound, as I can't see any way in which it would have helped. As cars are so expensive any fluctuation in exchange rates would have a large effect.

12/40

How to score full marks

- Typical mark allocation for this question: Content 8, Application 8, Analysis 8 and Evaluation 16. Total 40.
  Marks awarded for Mark's response: Content 2, Application 2, Analysis 5 and Evaluation 3. Total 12 marks.

- This appears to be a classic case of a candidate who has read the essay title and thought 'ooh yes, I know about this one' and proceeded to write their response. This is not always the best approach! In this instance, Mark has shown some good knowledge of the subject and the exchange rate mechanism but he **has only developed one point and only provided one side of the argument**. This is probably because **he has not correctly identified the triggers or signals in the question and so has not correctly focused his answer**.

- Mark is correct in that the question is asking him to analyse how the high value of the pound could have contributed to the factory closures. However, the key words 'to what extent' in the question signal that the question is also asking him to consider what factors **other than** the one given could have been likely contributory factors. **Then, the evaluation would consist of weighing up the likely import of the various factors outlined to arrive at a measured conclusion as to which of the factors would be the most relevant.**

- This highlights the need to **plan your response** before starting to write so that you are certain that your answer matches the demands of the question. Through lack of planning, repetition, and consequent inability to evaluate, Mark's answer was never going to get more than basic marks.

- Mark should have considered other factors such as:
  - How expensive and productive UK workers are compared to their foreign counterparts.
  - The age of the factories that were shut. It makes most sense to shut your oldest least efficient sites.
  - The impact of the euro and stable/common currency values across European factories.
  - Overcapacity in the car market and the effect of falling UK car prices.

A consideration of one or more of these additional points would have allowed Mark to evaluate and reach a judgement.

 This question also demonstrates the necessity of being aware of business news stories. Both these factory closures and the reasoning given by the companies were covered extensively by various media formats. Candidates who were conscious of this and used the information in their responses would have gained higher marks than Mark.

Don't forget ...

It is well worth spending a little time planning your essay carefully. You have a choice of questions so before you start, make sure you can provide a balanced (two-sided) argument.

Answer the question set. Essays often have trigger/signal words that you need to respond to. Direct your answer at these triggers and you will present more focused arguments.

All essay question have the majority of their marks weighted toward evaluation (40% of the total for AQA candidates). This is a skill that you need to develop through practice and the best way to do this is by answering past questions.

Real-life experience can be just as useful as classroom knowledge. Gaining marks on the application skill for essays can often mean relating to real-life situations or news stories. Keep up-to-date by reading newspapers, business magazines and watching business programmes.

Make sure you leave enough time to answer the essay question fully. Many candidates spend far too long on the report section. Remember they are both worth equal marks.

Remember business studies topics are interrelated. A good tactic for essays is to try and consider the financial, marketing, production, people or economic implications of the title you are given to discuss.

To gain high marks on level-of-response marking (see page 6), **try to develop two or three in-depth arguments rather than a series of superficial points**. Never provide a bullet point list in response to an essay question. This will only gain level one marks for content, and maybe application, but nothing for analysis or evaluation.

Key points to remember

- Candidates are often told that a **good essay** has three main sections: introduction, analysis and conclusion. This may well be true, but in a time-constrained environment such as an exam **do not waste time with a lengthy introduction or re-writing the question title**. Similarly telling the examiner 'how' you are going to approach the question is using up valuable time without achieving anything constructive. It is perfectly acceptable, in fact advisable, to just get straight into the question with your first main line of argument.

- It is important to have a coherent structure. **Your answer should be written in continuous prose, with well-defined paragraphs**. Each paragraph should outline and then develop each point you want to make, perhaps including judgements about its validity, relevance or likelihood. One of the most important aspects of business studies is **timescale**. For example, cash flow problems are immediate whereas profits are more long term.

- **Balance your answer**. There is very rarely only one viewpoint involved in any given business or economic situation, Give due consideration to at least two differing aspects of every essay title. This is exactly what the command word '**discuss**' means.

- Very often the answer to an essay question is that '**it depends**'. It is not enough to just state this – it must be developed. What are the most important dependent factors and why? Is it, for example, the type of product that the company sells or perhaps its market type? A solution that may be appropriate for one firm may be wholly unsuitable for another. **Be specific**; factors such as the market sector, size, experience and legal form of the company will all have an influence on how appropriate a given conclusion is.

- **Business Studies is not a specific subject – it is an amalgamation of many**. In-depth knowledge of a specific area drawn from other subjects that you may be studying such as Economics, Accounting or Sociology (as well as many others) may well be relevant, but be careful not to use these lines of argument in a business context – focus on the effects to the business, not a general discussion of theories. Candidates who achieve a high grade in Business Studies tend to have a good knowledge of all the component parts of Business Studies and are able to **provide a response which highlights how these aspects fit together in an integrated approach**.

Do ...	Don't ...
... question the validity of any statements made in the question. Are they facts or opinions, for example?	... waste time defining business terminology in the title and writing an introduction. This will only gain very few marks.
... start a new paragraph for each new point or each new skill you are demonstrating. This makes it very clear to the examiner how you are progressing.	... begin essays with statements like "Yes, I agree completely". This has a tendency to unbalance your arguments.
... make sure you are answering the question. Identify the triggers and focus your answer on these aspects.	... make sweeping statements that all businesses, customers or employees will react or behave in certain ways. This is very rarely accurate. Better language is to state things may, might or could happen.

Questions to try

1   The Internet is starting to revolutionise business. To what extent will business benefit from such a revolution?   [40 marks]

2   'It is impossible to predict accurately the future business environment, so there is little point in a business drawing up strategic plans.' Discuss this view.   [40 marks]

3   Quist Ltd. is a component manufacturer with a single factory that is currently operating at close to full capacity. It is considering whether to bid for a major new contract. Discuss the factors it would need to consider before deciding whether to go ahead with making a bid for the contract.   [40 marks]

4   Recently many British-based manufacturers have been transferring production overseas. To what extent is this trend desirable?   [40 marks]

Note: in the actual AQA paper 5W exam candidates must choose one from the above four.

Examiner's hints
- **Question 1** This is a question that requires more thought than is at first apparent. The **trigger here is 'to what extent'** which signals you need to consider how **businesses do and do not benefit.** Before you start, take a few minutes to consider exactly how a business can use the Internet – it's not just for selling goods. Can you evaluate whether particular categories of products or perhaps business sectors benefit more than others?
- **Question 2** Is there really 'little point' in strategic planning? **The command word 'discuss' is the trigger here** as it signals that you need a sound consideration of the **benefits and drawbacks** of producing strategic plans. **You also need to evaluate** whether strategic planning is more important to some firms than others.
- **Question 3** Break this question into its essential triggers. What **factors** should a **component** manufacturer consider **before** bidding for a **major** new contract, bearing in mind they are close to **full capacity**?
- **Question 4** The trigger words here are again **'to what extent'** and **'desirable'**. Whether or not something is desirable depends very much on who you are. Focus on this aspect when producing your answer and **you should be able to score high marks for evaluation.**

Answers to questions 1 and 4 can be found on pages 98–99.

5 | External Influences

Exam Question and Answer

A Quirky situation

The UK pasta giant Quirks has found business declining lately. Their products are mainly based around different types of dried pasta and they concentrate on supplying the supermarket own brand labels as well as producing a few of their own well recognised value brands such as the 'Farm Shopper' label, distinguishable by its highly visible blue and red striped packaging.

In their 2002 company report, Quirk's Mission Statement is given as:

'Quirks as a company will strive to provide quality low-cost products, whilst maintaining a prominent market position and meeting the needs of our stakeholders.'

The Managing Director, Emma Dixon, believes that this mission statement is not being met as a direct result of the decline in sales figures over the last three quarters. Primarily she feels, like many other manufacturing organisations, that a large proportion of the cause of this decline can be laid at the feet of the UK's currently comparatively high interest rates (see Appendix A). Whilst it may be true that areas of the economy such as housing and the high street retailers are experiencing a period of steady, if slow, growth, manufacturing enterprises have encountered consecutive quarters of declining trade and fear a deepening recessionary period looms on the horizon.

Speaking at the annual AGM, Emma unveiled the company's strategic plan:

'In view of the recent financial returns it is envisaged by the Board that an organisation such as Quirks should be forward thinking and pro-active toward its own perceived future. Although Quirks may be considered to be a major player in the UK dried pasta products market, it remains true to say that on a wider scale by European standards we are still only a medium-sized operator.

It is our intended plan that some of our profit resources should be diverted from their current investment programmes into an EU wide development plan. Currently European sales comprise 20% of our annual turnover and it is foreseen that in order to provide Quirks with a safe and secure financial future, that this needs to expand by another 20% over the next three years. A company such as Quirks should not be so heavily reliant on the performance of our domestic economy alone.

In conjunction with this, the Board would also like to recommend this course of action as a means to counteract some of the current expansion programmes being undertaken by our EU counterparts.'

Emma Dixon was speaking after announcing to shareholders that pre-tax profits for the second half of the year had seen a decline of 8% in comparison to the first half figures as well as a fall of 11.4% in comparison with the previous year.

As a result of Emma's speech at the AGM, Quirks' share price recovered slightly from its year low of £2.64 to £2.74 per share. Pundits commented that a major influence on business performance is confidence and that, with reported declines in manufacturing output across sectors and regions, a forward-thinking approach such as that outlined had been welcomed by City analysts.

However, the Board of Quirks are not in unanimous agreement as to the cause of the recent troubles. Robert Williams, the company's long-term Financial Director and renowned for his cautionary approach, is not convinced that Emma's are the only explanations for the company's current problems nor that increasing overseas sales is the only, or even most appropriate, plan to follow.

Appendix A

Comparison of UK and Overseas percentage base interest rates for the previous financial year

	UK %	Euro zone %
Quarter 1	4.5	3.75
Quarter 2	4.25	3.75
Quarter 3	4.00	3.50
Quarter 4	4.00	3.50

1   Quirks want to employ a strategy of increasing sales achieved from overseas sources. Assess the strengths and weaknesses of this approach.   [14 marks]

2   Discuss the other strategies that Quirks could employ to combat a recessionary period in the UK market.   [16 marks]

3   Discuss the likely effects that the EU may have on the competitive position of a business like Quirks.   [16 marks]

4   Evaluate the effect the comparatively high interest rates might have had on the competitiveness of Quirks.   [18 marks]

NICK'S ANSWERS

1 Quirks want to employ a strategy of increasing sales achieved from overseas sources. Assess the strengths and weaknesses of this approach. [14 marks]

I think that there are several key points that need to be considered.

Strengths

First, by increasing their level of sales achieved, Quirks are probably also going to increase the level of profit that they make. It reasonably follows that the more goods you sell the more profit you should make.

Secondly, making and selling more should also achieve economies of scale, i.e. the bigger you become, the better you become. This again would help them secure greater profits.

An advantage of expanding overseas is that it offers the company new and much larger markets to aim at, with lower risk compared to a strategy such as diversification.

Weaknesses

There are also several drawbacks with this plan.

It may prove to be very expensive. Quirks will have to promote its products to foreign supermarkets and customers to convince them to buy more. This is likely to involve a lot of expense especially as Emma says this development is to take three years.

Also, the question does not say what capacity the company has. If they increase overseas sales they may need to also expand their production. This again will be expensive, as they will need new machinery, staff and training — all of which would cost a lot of money.

So there are several advantages and several disadvantages. They may achieve bigger markets and more sales but it is going to cost them.

(7/14)

How to score full marks

Nick's answer to this question is a good example of **a very common mistake** made by candidates (especially on AQA paper 6). Nick has outlined the strengths and weaknesses but it is obvious that he has looked at the mark allocation for this and the other questions and decided that as question 1 is only worth 14 marks then it only requires an explanatory response. **He has, though, failed to recognise that the command word 'assess' signals that this is actually an evaluative question.**

All the questions on AQA paper 6 require evaluation irrespective of the marks available. This is a typical marking grid for this type of question on paper 6: Content 3, Application 2, Analysis 3 and Evaluation 6.
Marks awarded for Nick's response: Content 3, Application 2, Analysis 2 and Evaluation 0. Total 7.

To achieve full marks for this question, **Nick would need to have analysed each of his points in more depth, especially the one involving economies of scale**. He would need to have explained what types of economies could be experienced and how they would affect the company.

Nick would also have needed to provide some evaluation. He could have discussed:

- the degree of risk involved (as Quirks have experience in this field already, perhaps it's not that great a step)
- the idea that dried pasta products are very similar across all countries so that the level of economies of scale that could be achieved might well outweigh any costs as the products are basic and there are few, if any, differences required in manufacturing products for the domestic or foreign market.

---

2 Discuss the other strategies that Quirks could employ to combat a recessionary period in the UK market.

[16 marks]

One of the ways a company can typically cope better during a recessionary period is to lower the quality of the products it produces, i.e. they can start to produce a more inferior version. This should help to protect the level of sales being made by the company because during a recession people's incomes fall as they lose their jobs. People with less income will buy products that are cheaper, particularly basic food items like Quirks. So one course of action they could take is to try to start to appeal to the cheaper end of the market. This follows the theory of income elasticity.

Secondly, they could increase the level of their expenditure on advertising and promotion to encourage consumers to buy more, such as special offers like buy one get one free. I appreciate though that this is not always easy as increasing advertising is expensive and therefore may cause the company to actually lose money overall. However, the objective during a recessionary period is more geared toward survival than profits so perhaps this doesn't matter.

A third tactic would be to rationalise operations. This involves cutting back on the workforce and productive capacity so that it matches the level of demand during the recession. So, although Quirks may not be making as much profit as before the recession, they would not be carrying excess costs such as workers and machines standing around idle. A big drawback of this approach is that when the economy starts to recover you may not be able to get your workforce back again. However, it might allow the company to combat and survive recession.

A final option would be to drop the price of their products; this is similar in a way to my first point but involves price elasticity instead of income. Here, though, the mechanism is that the product stays the same but it just becomes cheaper for customers so they will continue to buy it even if they have a lower disposable income. The company can then keep its workforce as they are still running at the same level of capacity; they are just making less money per product. So long as the company doesn't make a loss, and a company the size and experience of Quirks should know how much to sell their products for, they should be all right.

11/16

How to score full marks

Following on from Nick's previous answer he has made a similar error here, though perhaps not so extreme. From his response, it is obvious that he feels an **analytical response** is required. Compared to his first answer, **his points are much more developed and focused on the idea of the core of the question, i.e. how to combat recession.** He uses a good style of a separate paragraph for each point and discusses each possibility in some depth. **Nevertheless the weakness still lies in the fact that he has failed to provide full evaluation of his arguments.**

A typical marking grid would be: Content 3, Application 3, Analysis 4 and Evaluation 6. Marks awarded for Nick's response: Content 3, Application 3, Analysis 4 and Evaluation 1. Total 11.

Nick has again **tried to relate his answer in several cases to Quirks actual circumstances** and the products that they sell, so **he receives full marks for application.** He has definitely raised relevant points and **provided analysis.** He has, however, **only achieved 1 evaluation mark** for the judgement he makes about the degree of risk associated with a particular option in his final paragraph.

It would have been relatively easy for Nick to achieve more evaluation marks. For example, Nick's argument in paragraph one is valid and encompasses some relevant business theory. If he had finished by making a judgement that perhaps this really wasn't an option, as Quirks already appear to service this inferior end of the market, he would have gained evaluation marks.

Equally he would have achieved some evaluation marks if he had stated that his third option – rationalising operations – is more appropriate if the company regards any recessionary effects as being medium- to long-term rather than short-, whereas short-term effects could well be combated with increased advertising and promotion.

An evaluative argument could also have been developed around paragraph 3 regarding the type of labour required by Quirks. It is far easier to find low-skilled workers than high-, perhaps making this approach a more viable option for Quirks than for other businesses that need highly skilled workers.

3 Discuss the likely effects that the EU may have on the competitive position of a business like Quirks. [16 marks]

I think the effects of the EU on a business like Quirks are probably going to be disastrous. It says in the case study that Quirks really aren't that big compared to other competitors and as such they will be at a disadvantage and perhaps at risk of takeover, especially as a European competitor looking the other way may decide to use Quirk's brand names and contacts as a springboard into the UK market place. Larger competitors will have greater advertising budgets as well and so will be able to out promote a company like Quirks and will no doubt end up stealing their customers.

Another thing is that although I can understand the Managing Director's plan, these larger European competitors aren't just going to let Quirks waltz in and take their customers. They are going to fight back and perhaps at worst try to take the UK market away from them as well.

The main point is that, as I said in my previous answer, the demand for these types of products is based on price and income. Dried pasta is really a very basic product and customers will make their decisions based on what they can afford, and not on advertising. Bigger EU competitors are likely to have cheaper prices than Quirks and so be able to undercut them, or perhaps have greater reserves so they could launch a price war. Either way, it is not good news for Quirk's.

A final argument is that in Europe Quirks are going to face the problem of fluctuating exchange rates and transaction costs that their foreign counterparts do not face. This again really implies that their (the foreigners') costs will be lower and Quirks are going to suffer.

So I think the effect of the EU is going to be a major problem for Quirks and I suppose I agree with the Finance Director that they perhaps need to do something else such as invest in the most up-to-date machinery.

13/16

How to score full marks

- Typical marks awarded for this question: Content 3, Application 3, Analysis 4 and Evaluation 6.
  Marks awarded for Nick's response: Content 3, Application 2, Analysis 3 and Evaluation 5. Total 13.

- **This time Nick has made a series of judgemental and therefore evaluative arguments.** However, **the focus is very one-sided.** He needed to also consider ways in which competitiveness might have been **enhanced**, such as benefiting from economies of scale. Although Nick has written about this in a previous response, don't be afraid to use the same line of reasoning again in a different answer if it's going to gain you marks.

- So, to gain full marks, Nick would have had to outline at least one point expressing how Quirk's competitive position could be improved. He would also have needed **to express and justify, in a concluding paragraph, an opinion regarding which of his arguments he thought the most relevant**.

4 Evaluate the effect the comparatively high interest rates might have had on the competitiveness of Quirks. [18 marks]

Interest rates are effectively the cost of borrowing money and are set by the Bank of England in the UK and the European Central Bank in Frankfurt for the EU. From the case study data it can be seen that the UK's rates are higher than the EU's in every quarter given. As interest rates are the cost of borrowing money, they not only affect Quirks as a company but also its customers.

Firstly, as a company, Quirks will have increased the costs of any borrowed funds they have, i.e. they will have to start making higher repayments on any loans with variable rates such as a mortgage. Even if they don't have any borrowed funds themselves (unlikely for a big company) some of their suppliers will and they may increase their prices, thus affecting Quirks costs anyway. Higher costs are going to have the effect of making Quirks less competitive as they will have fewer profits to use for development or promotion. This is bound to be true as they do not have the ability to pass increased costs onto the consumer because their products will be price sensitive as they appeal to the bottom end of the market. If they put their price up customers will switch to cheaper ones so Quirks have no choice but to take the knock in profits.

Secondly, their customers too will have to pay back more on any funds they've borrowed, such as on their personal loans, cars or mortgages. Consumers these days buy many products on credit, from cars and computers to furniture and even clothes, so they will have to repay more and therefore they will spend less, again decreasing demand and profits for Quirks.

However, I actually think this last point is unlikely. As Quirks sell goods at the bottom end of the market they may actually see their level of sales increase as customers switch to buying the cheaper brands such as supermarket own labels or their 'Farm Shopper' one.

My judgement here is again that the Finance Director may be right as a rise in interest rates or recession shouldn't perhaps cause Quirks that many problems as they make basic goods. Nevertheless though, they may face some increased costs and so have slightly lower profit margins.

Finally, there is the effect on exchange rates. If interest rates go up then the pound will become stronger.

12/18

How to score full marks

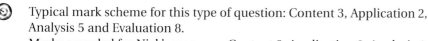
Typical mark scheme for this type of question: Content 3, Application 2, Analysis 5 and Evaluation 8.
Marks awarded for Nick's response: Content 3, Application 2, Analysis 4 and Evaluation 3. Total 12.

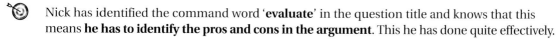
Nick has identified the command word '**evaluate**' in the question title and knows that this means **he has to identify the pros and cons in the argument**. This he has done quite effectively.

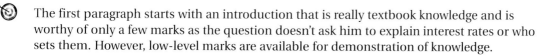
The first paragraph starts with an introduction that is really textbook knowledge and is worthy of only a few marks as the question doesn't ask him to explain interest rates or who sets them. However, low-level marks are available for demonstration of knowledge.

In subsequent paragraphs Nick develops his points and the good aspect of this is that Nick relates his line of argument to how rising interest rates could **improve** as well as decrease a company's competitive position, which is really what the question is asking for. This is a good example of an answer that considers **both sides of the argument and remains centred on the core of the question**. Nick has also realised that his answer will require some form of judgement.

To gain full marks, Nick would have needed to leave more time to consider the effect cheaper imports and more expensive exports would have had, and the relative importance of these effects.

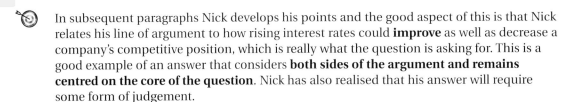

Don't forget ...

External influences questions form part of your **synoptic assessment so arguments from all the topic areas are relevant** in constructing your responses.

The focus of the unit six case study is often concerned with international businesses and markets. **You need to be aware of the main determinants of international competitiveness and the importance of an integrated approach to business**. This is vital in achieving full marks on synoptic assessment.

The information in the case study is there to help you. Not all of it will be relevant to the exact questions asked. However, **you need to be able to make basic assumptions about the type of business, type of market, number of competitors and possible income and price elasticities of the product**. This will help you make judgements about what likely actions or responses might be.

Make sure you **read the case study carefully**. A good technique is to skim it quickly through once to get the general idea. Then **re-read it carefully highlighting important points**. You'll often find that any numerical data in the text is there for a reason.

For AQA candidates, **all the questions on the case study exam require you to evaluate. Evaluation relies on reaching a reasoned judgement**, stemming from your own arguments given in your answer. Evaluation that relies on statements or assertion that something is so, will gain few if any marks.

External influences questions will invariably have some connection with **government actions**. Avoid using political answers or making political statements. Similarly pure economic theory will also gain few marks. The focus of the question is always about **how are businesses affected**, and your answers should **look at issues from the business point of view**.

To get top-level marks on many case study questions it is necessary to relate your answers to the context of the business and the scenario given. **Think about how situations affect the individual business you are given**.

A good technique is to **think how might different stakeholder groups be affected** by any situation and then consider their reactions. This will often provide you with insight into how the business itself will then be affected in turn. This is also a good way of approaching questions relating to business ethics.

Another tactic is to consider how Social, Legal, Economic, Political or Technological (**SLEPT**) factors could impact on the scenario given.

Economic opportunities and constraints

First you need to re-familiarise yourself with AS unit 3 topics such as: interest rates, exchange rates, inflation, unemployment and the business cycle as well as issues such as the labour market and workforce planning (see *Do Brilliantly AS Business Studies*). The focus is on how the changing economic environment provides businesses with opportunities or constrains their actions.

International competitiveness This area examines the ability of a company to compete with rival companies from overseas economies. International competitiveness is affected not only by external factors such as interest and exchange rates (covered in AS) but also by internal organisation and the integration of business factors to achieve an efficient organisation with desirable products.
Marketing – Develop products, inform customers, develop markets
Production – Efficient working practices, quality (e.g. BS ISO EN 9000), low cost
People – Motivated, participating, trained
Finance – Available, planned and budgeted, high quality

Economic growth This refers to the increase in the 'real' value of goods and services been produced by an economy. It is measured by a country's Gross Domestic Product (GDP). Growth encourages: investment, consumer spending, training and education. However it can result in: inflation, shortages of goods and labour and negative effects for inferior goods.

Growth also does not occur uniformly; some regions may benefit more than others, thus widening any disparities (north/south divide or the gap between rich and poor).

The European Union and overseas opportunities

This presents several areas for analysis:
- Single currency, stable exchange rates, free movement of goods and labour
- New markets, increased consumers, access to labour
- Increased competition
- Loss of UK jobs, cheaper labour overseas

You need to have an understanding of the roles and responsibilities of:
- European Commission – proposes European policy and legislation.
- Council of Ministers – agrees to adopt or reject legislation.
- European Parliament – advises the council on amendments to legislation and monitors the implementation of legislation and policies.
- European Central Bank – issues notes and sets the rate of interest for the Euro.
- European Court of Justices – oversees EU law and disputes between member states.

The single currency

Advantages	Disadvantages
Stable exchange rates between members. Leads to greater certainty, easier clarity of price information, better planning and decisions.	Greater price transparency means greater competition.
Cheaper costs. Transaction costs for changing currencies no longer apply.	Cost of changeover – tills, stationery, software. Consider the cost to a company like Poundland.

This area was also considered in *Do Brilliantly AS Business Studies* Chapter 5.

Key points to remember

Government policy

It is Government policy to achieve:
- Low unemployment
- Economic growth
- Low inflation
- Balance of payments

by using:
- Fiscal policy – the use of taxation and government spending to affect the level of economic activity and demand in the economy.
- Monetary policy – the use of interest rates and the supply of money to affect the level of activity and demand in the economy.

The focus is not on economic theory, but how businesses are affected. Remember that how a business is affected is determined by factors such as whether:
- It imports or exports or both
- It has luxury or inferior products
- It needs skilled or unskilled employees
- Its products are price elastic or price inelastic

Government intervention

This focuses on the involvement of the government in aspects of the economy that affect the environment in which businesses conduct their activities. Areas include:
- Legislation
- Grants, subsidies and support
- Price and Income controls
- Regional policies

The case for intervention

Can protect fledgling and/or companies of national importance

Can encourage activity in poorer regions

Protects workers and consumers

The case against intervention

Intervention such as legislation usually increases business bureaucracy and costs.

Freedom (*laissez faire* approach) promotes competition.

Encourages a more efficient use of resources as businesses are not protected by artificial subsidies.

Privatisation

This is the act of transferring ownership of state-owned and -controlled organisations to the private sector. Key factors include:
- Possibility of lower prices and better quality through greater competition.
- Privatised industries must become efficient and profitable to survive promoting efficiency and development.
- Large-scale redundancies through restructuring and rationalisation resulting in unemployment.
- Difficulties in funding investment for infrastructure projects e.g. railways
- Foreign ownership of industries of national importance.
- The re-distribution of profits through many small UK citizen shareholders.

Social and other factors

Social responsibility includes businesses being aware and acting on the following, **that are not legal requirements**:
- Responsibilities to employees – training and development and non-exploitation of non-EU employees
- Responsibilities to customers – awareness of attitudes and moral stance, provision of accurate information
- Responsibilities to communities – environmental issues, effect of business action on local economies
- Responsibilities to suppliers, shareholders, creditors etc.

Business can gain a much-improved image and custom from behaving responsibly. Alongside this they may also gain in productivity from happy and motivated workforce. However, in many cases, can the business afford to act in a responsible manner? They may be too small, competition may be too fierce, and the economy may be in a recession or slump. Alternatively, can they afford not to? Possibilities include losing employees and customers to other more responsible competing companies.

Pressure groups

These are defined as being groups of individuals who share a common interest and combine together to bring about change. They attempt to do this in several ways.
- Political lobbying
- Direct action

Pressure group action can be very damaging to large firms who attract media attention and are in the public eye. Action can damage their corporate image, lose customers or cause the government to impose fines or additional legislation, increasing costs. This is of particular importance in highly competitive markets.

Social auditing

This is an assessment of a company's achievement of its aims and objectives in relation to the impact its activities has had on its stakeholder groups, i.e. it measures the social and ethical stance of the business. A business can benefit from social auditing because, by reviewing its processes, it can identify areas of anti-social behaviour and eradicate them. This promotes corporate image and helps attract and retain employees and clients. It also makes the organisation consider the efficiency of its organisation by focusing on anti-social aspects such as waste and pollution, reduction of which could bring major cost savings, (this could also cost money as well) and attract grants or investors.

Question to try

As per the AQA paper 6, external influences forms part of the integrated synoptic case study. A question to try can therefore be found at the end of Chapter 6 (page 88).

Exam Question and Answer

Sunnydales

It had been a bitterly cold day and so far not a good one. Brian Collier, the owner operator of Sunnydales Ltd, (the other major shareholder being his wife) had just returned to his office after yet another round of less than encouraging talks with Chris Wells, his employees' union representative. Having removed his hat and gloves, he now warmed his hands round his usual morning brew and tried to puzzle out how he had arrived in this current situation.

As a young man Brian had moved from job to job, finally securing a position with the Lotus car manufacturer based in Norfolk. Here he trained as a fibreglass mould maker and finally ended up working for Team Lotus designing and making specialist moulds and parts for their various race cars, including Formula One during the 1970s. It was during this era that Brian first thought of his bright idea. Race cars typically use aerodynamically shaped wings and spoilers to reduce air friction and so produce less drag. This has two main effects: enhanced speed and lower fuel consumption. This led in the first instance to Brian designing and patenting an aerofoil to fit on the front of caravans to achieve similar effects and eventually grew into Sunnydales Caravans. He opened his current factory in 1979.

Sunnydales as a company is based on the idea of mass manufacturing a small range of caravan bodies and then using experienced craftsmen to hand tailor internal fixtures and fittings to the customer's exact requirements. Alongside this, Sunnydales caravans come with a large range of optional external accessories for both caravans and cars, all of which are designed to reduce aerodynamic drag or enhance stability whilst towing at speed. However, despite Brian's habit of patenting all his new ideas it doesn't seem long before competitors bring out rival products offered at a much lower price than Sunnydales can afford. This, coupled with the recent trend of customers shifting from caravan purchases to camper vans, has meant that Sunnydales has found itself gradually losing market share.

Brian, though, is not the sort of owner to stand still. In recent months he has commissioned designs for three camper van models, negotiated deals for the supply of engines, gearboxes and running gear as well as having employed an industrial architect, Graeme Affleck, and project manager, Alex McNair, to consider a complete factory overhaul. Brian's view is that if you can't beat them, join them, and as such intends to scale back caravan manufacture and replace it with basic mass-produced camper vans. This drastic change was brought about after an uncomfortable meeting with his accountant and financial manager, where they demonstrated through the use of decision trees and ratios that in its current situation Sunnydales would probably be forced to close in three years unless the decision to switch to a more cost efficient method of production was taken. Brian, faced with this reality, decided to take this as an opportunity and embarked on a major re-think of his entire business. He decided the following:

- Scale back on caravan manufacture and introduce a new range of camper vans.

- Switch from the old production line method of production to cell production on caravan manufacture.

- Introduce more automated systems and robots in the basic production of body panels for both caravans and camper vans.

- Re-design the factory layout to achieve a more efficient state of the art production process, including training and development of key employees.

- Add a new factory extension to house new automated paint bays for camper vans and also to include better staff facilities.

Brian is aware that the Sunnydales' reputation has been built upon a traditional culture of providing an excellent service to customers and using a highly experienced workforce to produce quality products. However, his opinion is that there's no reason why this should change despite the changes to the factory. Brian is at odds with the union who recognise that Brian's idea probably involves some redundancies or early retirements and a significant change in working practices, and so is offering considerable resistance to the proposed changes. What Brian seems unable to communicate is that he feels this is the only way of securing the long-term future of jobs and the company itself.

This, of course, is not the only conflict that exists between stakeholders. Another consideration is that in order to finance the proposed ideas Brian would have to take Sunnydales public and become a listed company on the Stock Exchange. Putting his personal feelings aside, Brian is prepared to sacrifice his ownership and goals to ensure the company's future and cannot understand why others appear to be so obstructive. The only people who appear to be on his side are his wife Sarah and his accountant, Chris Miller, who assures him that at this point in time becoming a plc is the right move for Sunnydales.

1   Consider the extent to which the aims of Sunnydales' stakeholder
    groups may come into conflict.   [14 marks]

2   Evaluate the use of decision trees in determining business strategies.   [16 marks]

3   Assess the ways in which Sunnydales could address the current
    business culture and the workforce's current attitude to change.   [16 marks]

4   To what extent might floating on the Stock Exchange be the right move
    for Sunnydales?   [18 marks]

SARAH'S ANSWERS

1 Consider the extent to which the aims of Sunnydales' stakeholder groups may come into conflict. [14 marks]

Given Brian's plans concerning his company, it is not surprising that many of the various stakeholder groups involved in his company are unhappy. What he's proposing to do doesn't seem to suit anyone, not even himself.

His employees are going to be unhappy, as highlighted by the difficulties he is having with the union rep. Not only is it proposed that there will be redundancies, although some early retirements may help reduce these, he is also proposing to break up established working patterns.

Other groups, such as customers, could be unhappy as Brian is proposing to change the products that he makes and the way he makes them. This means that many customers may no longer be able to get what they want, causing them to be unhappy.

As a private limited company, the only shareholders appear to be him and his wife. By going public this may conflict with their main aims of running and owning their own company. However, it does say that Brian believes this is the only way his company will survive. If the standard shareholder goal of profits is accepted, then this does fit in with what he wants, because if he doesn't complete his plan, then in a few years there will be no profit at all.

Therefore, although I can accept and recognise that different groups will have different problems, overall the survival of the company comes first, so I think that Brian is right to be doing what he is.

7/14

How to score full marks

- Although only worth 14 marks this question does **still require an evaluative response**. A typical marking for this question would be given as: Content 3, Application 2, Analysis 3 and Evaluation 6. Total 14.
  Marks awarded for Sarah's answer: Content 3, Application 2, Analysis 1 and Evaluation 1. Total 7.

- Sarah's answer to the question is rather weak in several respects. Firstly, **she has not really focused her answer on conflicts**, but rather on reasons why individual groups might be unhappy. Secondly, **her response is lacking in depth and analysis,** only developing her points to the explanatory level. Sarah does attempt some evaluation, but it is superficial at best and lacks insight, so she only scores 1 mark out of a possible 6 for evaluation.

- The best aspect of Sarah's answer is that **she has tried to relate her answer to the context of the question and the actual events that are taking place.**

- **The correct way to approach this question would have been to consider how the aims and goals of the various groups are actually called into conflict, with an analysis of why these conflicts exist.** Sarah does make a valid point that if the company actually doesn't survive then it will not be able to satisfy anybody's requirements, but she has expressed this poorly.

- A good line of argument would have been to **consider the various stakeholder groups' objectives in both the long- and the short-term** to arrive at a conclusion about whether or not these conflicts would be resolved if a longer perspective were to be taken.

2 Evaluate the use of decision trees in determining business strategies. [16 marks]

Decision trees have some advantages and disadvantages in helping managers to make decisions.

Advantages include:
1 They make managers think about different courses of action that are open to them, and perhaps come up with ideas that they may not, at first, have thought of.
2 They consider a numerical result of each decision so the best option can be chosen.
3 Managers need to consider the risks and implications of each decision to assign probabilities to the options.

The best advantage is that different options can be compared scientifically and thus the risk of making the wrong decision is decreased.

However, they also have disadvantages:
1 They are not 100% accurate. Managers can introduce bias through their own preferences.
2 Collecting accurate information can be costly and time consuming.
3 They don't take into account non-financial factors.

In summary, they are useful and provide a good basis for comparing options, but they are only as accurate as the information provided and, like any decision-making tool, should not be used just on their own to make major decisions.

5/16

How to score full marks

This response is of a variable quality. Sarah has **followed the golden rules of considering both sides and has tried to arrive at a reasoned judgement** at the end of it. The problem lies in her style of answering the question. If you use numbered points as opposed to writing a piece of continuous prose, you give yourself less chance to develop points in depth and introduce evaluation.

The marks available for this question would be: Content 3, Application 3, Analysis 4 and Evaluation 6. Total 16.
Marks awarded for Sarah's answer: Content 3, Application 0, Analysis 1 and Evaluation 1. Total 5.

Sarah's response has several content points, more than enough to gain all the content marks as she has also developed them slightly. However, she has not made any attempt to put her answer in context, that is, to apply it to the scenario. **She has given a theoretical textbook answer only, which is why she receives 0 marks for application.**

She also **does not analyse the implications or knock-on effects of the points she has raised**. Perfect opportunities to do this arise in several places. For example, Sarah could have considered the additional benefits to be gained from considering different courses of action such as enhanced communication and discussion. Alternatively, she could have considered the trade-off between the cost of gathering data and the benefit to be derived from it.

Sarah's evaluation in the last paragraph is correct but simplistic. Her arguments should have been constructed considering the timescale involved. For example, the further into the future predictions are made, the less accurate they will be. Sarah states that decision trees should not be used on their own, and indeed from the case study they are not. The company is also using ratio analysis, but is this enough? Can human implications and impacts be judged by financial criteria? Is the decision facing Sunnydales one that is easy to quantify? All these issues should have formed part of the **evaluation in relation to the actual scenario**.

3 Assess the ways in which Sunnydales could address the current business culture and the workforce's current attitude to change. [16 marks]

It is obvious from the case study that Brian is really actually only trying his best and wants the best for everybody concerned and I think it is a real shame that his workforce and the union are being uncooperative. However, it does say in the case study that Brian opened the factory in 1979. This is a long time ago and it also says that he uses traditional methods, so it is not surprising really that, after such a long period of time, the workers don't want to change. I think to get them to change is going to be really difficult.

The best way to actually change the culture of the organisation and get rid of the resistance though would be to talk to the employees directly, instead of through the unions. Brian should call a large meeting and explain to the workforce what is going on, what is going to happen if they don't do something, that is, everyone loses their job eventually, and what he's decided to do about it so at least the company can carry on trading and become more successful in the future.

He could also try to get the workers more involved in the process by using delegation, participation, quality circles or the like as these will help the workers be less resistant. It says he wants to introduce cell production, so perhaps he should tell the workers what this is and how much they're going to like it. Also he can tell them about the new facilities.

If Brian actually explains things by having a meeting, I'm sure the workers will listen, as it seems he wants to try and do the right thing.

9/16

How to score full marks

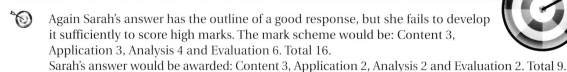

Again Sarah's answer has the outline of a good response, but she fails to develop it sufficiently to score high marks. The mark scheme would be: Content 3, Application 3, Analysis 4 and Evaluation 6. Total 16.
Sarah's answer would be awarded: Content 3, Application 2, Analysis 2 and Evaluation 2. Total 9.

Sarah's first paragraph is very limited in content. However, she does raise an interesting point – the length of time they have been working in this manner. **This would have made a good evaluation point** to develop – the fact that there are no quick fix solutions and that to change culture takes time. Sarah does address this slightly and so receives a limited mark for basic evaluation.

Paragraph two is much better. Perhaps the initial judgement that a meeting is the best way is a bit presumptuous but, in Sarah's defence, she does develop the point and try to add some context. Again, though, **this should have been developed in much greater depth.** She could have discussed the benefits of getting the factory workers involved in the re-design work or the fact that employees may benefit from re-training and higher skills, all of which are motivational factors.

In paragraph three Sarah makes a common error. All the factors she has listed are relevant points but **she needed to analyse several of these in depth** – how would they have helped change the culture, what benefits do the employees get that will make them want to change? This would then have provided Sarah with several lines of argument from which to be able to **evaluate** which method would be the best or the pros and cons of how long each might take. This would have allowed her to gain the marks for analysis and evaluation that she missed out on.

4 To what extent might floating on the Stock Exchange be the right move for Sunnydales? [18 marks]

The main advantage for Brian and his company of doing this is that it will provide the company with the money it needs to put all the new plans into practice. It will also probably make Brian quite rich. The good thing is, though, that this way the company raises the money without having to borrow it from a bank or venture capitalist and so does not have to pay any interest. This is likely to be quite significant, because with all the plans Brian has, he probably needs a large amount of money, so the interest on borrowed money could be extortionate. In this way the company gets an injection of cash effectively for free. Finally, the fact that the company has not borrowed anything means that it doesn't end up being highly geared or more at risk. The case study does not say if the company has borrowed anything already. Perhaps they have, which is why Brian needs to sell it as they could not borrow any more.

Another point is that to become a plc may well involve a lot of publicity and Sunnydales could benefit from this, as they may become better known. Certainly being able to invest in cheaper production processes and lowering cost means that there should be more for the advertising they are going to need to launch the new range of camper vans.

However, it is not all rosy. You don't just become a limited company — the cost of becoming one is very high. As I mentioned before, they are probably going to have to advertise to attract shareholders and produce a magazine called a prospectus and this will be very expensive. The problem here is that even though Sunnydales may want to be a plc, it doesn't just happen. People may not buy their shares. Then they will have gone through all this expense for nothing and the company will be even worse off as they will have spent the money for no gain.

The major drawback though is to Brian. He will effectively lose total control of his business as any new shareholders will want a say in how it is run and they may not agree with Brian's ideas. Thus the plan to save the business may end up costing Brian his position. This really depends on how many of the shares Brian sells to the public and how many he keeps himself. But given all his plans I imagine he needs to sell quite a lot to raise the money he needs.

The question asks whether this the right time. Well perhaps it isn't perfect, but I don't see any other option. The company needs the money to survive and this is the only way to raise it without getting massively into debt. Brian seems willing to go ahead with the decision and he has discussed it with his accountant, so really he has had good advice. Although there is a risk, I don't think the accountant would have advised him to do this if he thought it would end up ruining the company. Perhaps he could ask employees to become shareholders. This would help raise the money and get them more involved and motivated into helping the business be a success.

How to score full marks

🎯 A question of this type would have the following mark scheme: Content 3,
2, Analysis 5 and Evaluation 8. Total 18.
Sarah's answer would have been awarded: Content 3, Application 2, Analysis 5 and
Evaluation 7. Total 17.

🎯 In this instance Sarah has provided an exemplary answer and has obviously left herself sufficient
time to answer this last, high mark question well. **She has provided four lines of argument, two
from each side. She has developed each point in depth,** looking at the further implications of the
decisions on aspects of the business. The best example of this is in paragraph one.

🎯 She has **related her answer to the scenario given** by exploring why the company needs to raise the
money and also why this may or may not be the best way. Sarah is also **including evaluation in her
arguments**, such as judging the degree of finance needed and what happens to gearing and risk.

🎯 **The final paragraph is a good demonstration of how to gain high marks for evaluation.** Sarah draws
all her arguments together, explaining how and why she has reached her conclusion, again putting
her response in context. Finally, she finishes with an excellent and highly relevant suggestion.

Don't forget ...

The synoptic case study paper is the final A2 paper. Arguments drawn from Marketing, Finance and Accounting, People and Operations Management, External Influences and Objectives and Strategy are all valid responses to questions.

Make sure you leave enough time to answer the final question on the synoptic case study, as this will usually be worth the most marks (usually 18 marks for AQA). The final question will often be worth up to 25% of the total paper. By leaving insufficient time to answer you are severely limiting your chances of a high overall grade.

Don't use bullet-pointed lists or a plan layout when trying to gain marks if short of time. Usually an extended piece of prose will take less time to write and gain you more marks as you develop a relevant point and move through the response levels.

Always try to make your answers refer to the circumstances of the business or situation you have been presented with. Marks are always available for context or application. Alongside this, it makes achieving higher order evaluation marks easier as you can then make a specific reasoned judgement about the most important areas that influence or impact upon the scenario given.

The information in the case study is there to help you. In many case studies there will be supporting charts or tables of data. Pay particular attention to these. They may provide valuable clues about market trends, competition or the state of the economy. **This helps you to make informed judgements and gain marks for evaluation.**

Despite different mark allocations, **all the questions on Paper 6 for AQA candidates require you to demonstrate evaluation in your answers**.

The focus of synoptic questions is always about **how the business in the case study will be affected or how it should react**, and your answers should **look at issues from the business's point of view**.

Try to remember key areas that may have an influence on decisions. Use the mnemonic **SLEPT** – Social, Legal, Economic, Political and Technological.

A good technique for dealing with synoptic questions is to consider the business as an environment – it is a whole, not a series of unrelated parts.

Objectives and strategy

For AQA candidates this module is used as the basis for synoptic assessment (pages 84–87). Many of the areas contained within this section of the specification have been considered in the preceding chapters of this book and in **Do Brilliantly AS Business Studies**. Therefore, only key new aspects are considered here. Signposts and links to other areas of the specification are provided in the synoptic assessment section and should be read in conjunction with these key points.

Impact on firms of a change in size

Overtrading occurs when a firm grows without securing the finance necessary to fund this growth. It places huge strains on its working capital and cashflow position. Firms not only need to finance plans for expansion but also the day-to-day requirements of increased stocks and wages. Thus the risk of overtrading is that firms can run out of cash and be forced into liquidation.

Retrenchment occurs when firms are deliberately reducing the scale of their operations. This does not always indicate a firm in trouble. Companies may reduce scale to:
a) Get rid of peripherals and concentrate on core activities where it has most expertise and market power.
b) End production of lines which are no longer profitable (e.g. fashion and technologies change, IBM no longer need typewriter factories).
c) Achieve a more manageable size and remove diseconomies of scale, thus achieving lower unit costs even though a smaller than previous size.

Takeovers and mergers Often the fastest way to achieve growth is the external acquisition of another company. A takeover occurs when one company gains decision-making control over another. By contrast a merger is when companies join together to form one new unified operation. These can occur in three ways:
a) **Vertical** The firms involved are at different stages of the production process or sectors of the economy (e.g. a secondary manufacturer joins with a primary raw material producer).
b) **Horizontal** The firms involved are at the same stage of the production process or sector of the economy (e.g. a retailer joins with a retailer – Lloyds and TSB or Wal-Mart and ASDA).
c) **Conglomerate** This occurs when firms from diverse markets and operations join together (e.g. a company making fizzy drinks buys a radio station).

Benefits include: lower costs, new markets, spreading risk and economies of scale.
Drawbacks include: lack of experience, diseconomies of scale and conflicting cultures.

Business objectives

- **Mission statement** This is a document detailing the overall aims of the company. Its purpose is to provide focus and direction for employees so all aspects of the business work together. The mission statement is used to set objectives. However, it must be realistic and actually used or else it becomes a wasted and costly paper exercise.

- **Organisational culture** This comprises the attitudes, beliefs and decision-making process of the business. Types of cultures include:
  - **Power or club culture** – relies on the power of the owner or directors, who share like views and recruit similar minded people.
  - **Role cultures** – the delineation of the business into strict hierarchies and clearly defined jobs roles.
  - **Task cultures** – emphasis is on getting particular jobs or projects done.
  - **Innovative cultures** – a company that recognises change and embraces it.
  - **Conservative culture** – a company that likes to maintain its traditional approach.
  - **People culture** – the people in the business are more important than jobs or tasks.

  The organisational culture influences the way the business behaves, how employees work and the type of decisions they make.

Key points to remember

Business strategy

Scientific decision-making is the collection of data and the application of analytical systems or tools to help management arrive at a conclusion. It is costly and time consuming but is used to reduce the risk of errors and mistakes. It is highly dependent on the quality of the data provided but is in contrast to the application of management hunches or inspired guesswork through experience. (See section on synoptic assessment for individual topic examples of scientific models.)

Decision trees are a diagrammatic representation of possible options and financial outcomes with an estimate of the probability of their occurrence. Squares represent decisions to be made and circles, possible outcomes. This is a mathematical model used by managers to help in decision-making. Each possible outcome is represented by a probability (shown under the line) and a financial result (shown at the end of the line), the result for each decision is found by determining the sum of the products of each outcome for that decision. A line drawn across any option shows that it has not been chosen and has been discarded as a possibility.

Advantages	Disadvantages
Quantifiable analysis of decisions makes managers think decisions through and consider different options.	These are only estimates – actual probabilities are difficult to determine accurately.
Provides a numerical basis for comparison.	Doesn't consider non-financial factors that impact on decisions.

Corporate plan This is the long-term strategy to enable the company to achieve its objectives. From this, the functional areas derive their individual plans. Planning focuses managers on the future and provides direction for employees. It can also be used to aid communication and participation, but especially coordination, as a corporate plan forces the management to consider how the business's operations interrelate. However, it can be costly and time consuming, become out of date quickly and cause management to become inflexible – they stick to their plan and don't respond to a changing environment.

Contingency planning is the advance preparation of action plans to counteract unwanted or unlikely events, such as a fire in the factory or a severe recession. They can also be used to plan for positive contingencies like an unexpected surge in demand. This makes managers consider their operating environment as a whole and be pro-active in preparing for possible future developments, rather than being reactive to change and crisis management.

Synoptic assessment

Synoptic assessment is designed to test your knowledge and understanding of the subject as a whole, including how the different topic areas you have studied are related. For this reason the exam containing the synoptic assessment is taken at the end of your course – for AQA candidates, this is paper 6.

In this paper, **the synoptic element is assessed via a range of integrating themes**. These themes are chosen to represent the dynamic and interactive nature of the business world and assess all the aspects of your AS and A2 studies. Synoptic questions expect you to be able to recognise the relationship between what a business wants to achieve, its aims and objectives, and the way in which it operates in an uncertain and changing environment. To do this **you need to be able to devise, analyse and evaluate strategies that aim to anticipate, respond to and manage this changing environment.** Alongside this you need an awareness of how the business's actions affect stakeholder groups and the conflict of interests that exist between them. You need to be able to suggest and evaluate strategies for resolving stakeholder conflicts so that the business can achieve its goals. For AQA the three main integrating themes are:

- **Impact on firms of a change in size**
- **Business objectives**
- **Business strategy**

There is not space in this book to list every link between the integrating themes. Instead, some examples are given below of these links split into the topic areas you have studied. Each area considers:

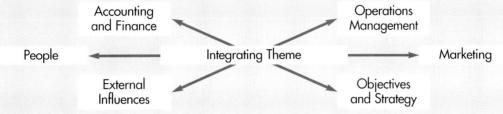

The lists provided are not exhaustive. **Consider each section below and try to add your own ideas of connections between topics.** This is also a good way of revising for your exam.

Changing size

This area examines the impact on firms of a change in size and a consideration of the management of problems a company may face as it grows.

Finance — **Links**

Internal versus external **sources of finance** for funding growth, choosing and evaluating the best sources; **cashflow problems** and the risk of **overtrading**; **investment appraisal** methods of differing projects.

People — **Links**

The effect on managers of changing spans of **control, delgation, communication** in the heirarchy and **participation** and co-ordination of a larger workforce;
a contrast of the benefits to be gained from growth given the possible loss of direction and control.

Production — **Links**

Economies versus diseconomies of scale; capacity utilisation of larger facilties and the effect on unit costs; sourcing supplies, identify **critical paths** for project completions and determining optimum **business location**.

Marketing — **Links**

Market analysis and the assessment of **market strategies**, e.g. the degree of risk associated with **diversification** or moving from a national to international market place. Factors include an examination of management experience and competition versus possible market size and increased profits.

External Influences — **Links**

The availability of government support such as grants and subsidies, as well as an awareness of the effect that a change in size has on a business's **ethical** and **social responsibilities**. The influence of the economic environment has on growth, i.e. raising finance and **interest rates, inflation** and business confidence or, alternatively, the influence of **exchange rates** and the **EU** on expanding internationally.

Objectives and Strategy — **Links**

Changes in size and operation often involve **mergers** or **takeovers**. Be aware of the effects of these actions of differing **stakeholder groups** and the conflict of interests between them. Growth can often mean a change in **legal form** – you need to consider the impact on costs and business operations, e.g. concerns over loss of control as a business moves from limited to plc status.

Business objectives and culture

The aims, mission statement, objectives and culture of an organisation exert an influence on all the differing component parts of the business and how they work together.

Finance

Financial objectives are paramount to many organisations and include not just making a profit but also, survival, breaking even and financial stability. There is often a trade-off between short-term profits or **cash flow managment** and the achievement of long-term strategic plans.

People

Knowing the purpose and goals of the business and their part in achieving them can unite a business's employees. The type of organisational culture can affect **motivation**, participation and **productivity,** e.g. a task versus people orientation or a conservative versus innovative approach. This is thus closely related to **management style** and motivation theories.

Production

The culture and objectives affect the way in which people work (**teamwork** versus specialisation) and how development takes place. A task **culture** focuses priority on the job not the people and innovative culture encourages new ideas. This influences implementation of techniques like **Kaizen** or **JIT** and affects how a company **manages change.**

Marketing

Heavily influenced by culture, e.g. if the business is customer focused and hence **market orientated**, this has a knock-on effect on the achievement of **marketing objectives** such as growth or improving market share.

External Influences

Society and its moral values exert pressure on firms to adjust the products that they make, the way they make them and even who they make them for. This area has close ties with the issues of business **ethics** and **social resposibility**. External influences like the **business cycle** will alter the short-term objectives set by a firm.

Objectives and Strategy

Stakeholder analysis, the long-term aims of focusing on the needs of stakeholders, can prove a rewarding strategy. Integrating the desires of customers, employees, owners, communities, etc. could result in a respected business, with motivated workers, efficient production methods and happy repeat purchasing customers generating **quality profits**. However, some long-term objectives are achievable only at the expense of some short-term stakeholder aims, e.g. growth may mean less profits for distribution as dividends as they are ploughed back into the business.

Business strategy

This focuses on the way in which businesses make decisions and the methods they employ to help them analyse and evaluate possibilities to determine future plans.

Finance

Investment appraisal techniques, ratio analysis, break-even, budgeting and variances – all can be employed to help reach comparitive judgements. However, all possess limitations as well as advantages, e.g. they take no consideration of non-financial factors.

People

Training and development, **recruitment** and **workforce planning**. A business needs to ensure that it has the correct workforce (now and in the future) to enable it to carry out its plans.

Production

Uses models such as **critical path analysis** or the examination of **product life cycles**, as well as examining methods of **controlling stock** or types of production. The method of production used (**job, batch** or **flow**, for example) will depend in part on the objectives the company wants to achieve.

Marketing

Examines the use of the **marketing model** and **scientifc decision-making** processes and helps in the selection and collection of data for determining strategies. Employing **market analysis** tools such as **Ansoff's matrix** is useful in evaluating the comparative risk presented by differing strategies.

External Influences

Doesn't employ any mathematical models, but does require an awareness of UK and EU **legislation** when considering long-term plans. Alongside this is an appreciation of the influence of **political** or **technological change** on the business environment.

Objectives and Strategy

The two main decision-making tools employed in this area are **SWOT analysis** and **decision trees**. Managers use these tools extensively to help determine strategy. You need to be able to evaluate these methods taking into considering their main advantages and limitations.

Key point No single tool on its own should be the basis for determing a business's long-term strategy.

Odyssey plc

David Poole arrived early for the board meeting at Odyssey. As he took his seat at the head of the table, waiting for the other directors to arrive, his attention was caught by the poster on the wall opposite. He recognised it instantly, surprised to find it still holding a prominent place in the boardroom. The poster showed the firm's mission statement, still in the form agreed by the original directors when the business went public in 1991.

He read the text again:

Mission Statement

Odyssey plc

Odyssey owns and operates pubs throughout the UK.
We will adopt a uniformity of style to establish and develop our brand's position in the market.
We will consider the needs of our stakeholders.
We will strive to be leaders in our market.

'Things have changed in the decade since that statement was put together', he thought to himself. 'Indeed, I'm not sure it's a mission statement at all. It should be rewritten to show where we are today, and where we are going. But maybe it can wait until other things are sorted out first.'

At the time of the flotation, the business had been a stock market star. Then, as the customer tastes changed, it became apparent that Odyssey's success had a weak base. Over the next couple of years, customer numbers started to fall and the profits dwindled alarmingly. At the same time, David's enthusiasm for his work declined. He missed being involved in the day-to-day running of the pubs – he remembered fondly standing in as a barman in the Tycho Arms, his very first pub. He felt his job was now pushing paper and balancing the conflicting interests of the board, the shareholders and all the other groups who had a say in things. He complained that he was no longer in control of his own business and was finding it impossible to be involved in everything that was going on. Finally, in 1995, David decided to retire. He was sure that there were many things a wealthy 50-year-old could do to keep himself busy.

Odyssey appointed the dynamic Frances Bowman as Chief Executive to follow David. Already well thought of in the City, she vigorously expanded the business. Her strategy for the pubs was to decentralise by allowing each manager to furnish the pub to suit local tastes. A rolling programme of two-yearly refurbishment was introduced to keep the pubs fresh and up to date. This started to attract new, younger customers.

More radically, Frances also took Odyssey into the hotel business. She developed a string of cheap, no-frills establishments, aiming primarily at tourists from Germany and France who wanted a base for walking, climbing and other outdoor holidays in the UK. Sites were chosen in places such as the Lake District and Peak District. Many of these areas had quite high unemployment and Frances made plain her pleasure at the local economic benefits provided by Odyssey hotels. She appeared on several TV programmes to speak on the topic of the social responsibilities of business. Although the Board of Directors liked the free publicity for Odyssey, one or two had private concerns about whether Frances focused sufficiently upon the interests of shareholders.

Initially, the hotel business prospered. Marketing campaigns on the continent were especially successful, and the hotels were very profitable at a time when the number of tourists coming into the UK from Western Europe was high. Frances also believed that the hotels raised the profile of the whole firm, which she felt could only help its other operations.

In the last couple of years, though, the high value of the pound has led to a fall in the number of tourists from Western Europe. Although the hotels have still been breaking even, they are absorbing a great deal of capital and management time. Even the pubs have been performing less well, though still better than just prior to David's retirement. The most recent economic indicators suggest a build up of inflationary pressures in the economy, and the government is hinting that its economic strategy may change to make control of inflation a priority.

Despite the more difficult economic climate, market analysts feel Odyssey's problems are largely internal. One noted commentator has pointed out that many problems arose after Odyssey moved into the hotel business, a market previously unfamiliar to them. He questioned how far the firm as a whole was committed to the new direction developed by Frances. With concerns growing about the company's future, just 6 weeks ago Frances announced she was leaving to take a key role in the government's Department of Leisure.

With no obvious candidate to take over the role, last Monday the Board invited David Poole back to help his former business overcome its immediate difficulties and to set a path for the future. He seems to be setting about this new challenge with great enthusiasm. David was never really in favour of the move to hotels, and so is considering selling them off to refocus the business on the pub trade he knows so well. He has already held informal talk with a multinational company, Clarke's Discovery Holidays, which is willing to make an initial offer of £5m to buy Odyssey's hotel division.

David believes the hotels can only be a success in their present form if the value of the pound drops significantly. If the pound's value doesn't fall one possible action is to keep the hotels and target customers in the United States, where the pound has been weak against the dollar. David glances again at his notes for the meeting, including a decision tree reflecting the current situation (see Appendix A). After all this time, he feels quite nervous about his first Board meeting for a decade. His thoughts are interrupted as his colleagues start to arrive. The future is about to begin.

Appendix A

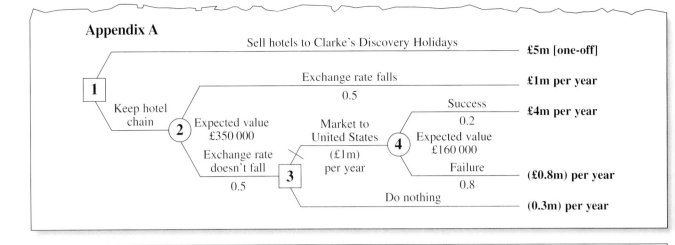

1 David Poole believes the original mission statement of Odyssey is no longer appropriate for the firm. To what extent might the firm benefit from a re-writing of the mission statement? [14 marks]

2 Discuss whether the Directors were right to be concerned about the apparent interest shown by Frances in social responsibilities. [16 marks]

3 It is believed that the government will now make the control of inflation a priority in its economic policies. Assess the impact this may have on Odyssey plc. [16 marks]

4 On the basis of the decision tree in Appendix A and any other relevant factors, consider whether Odyssey should accept the offer from Clarke's Discover Holidays. [16 marks]

5 David Poole is determined that Odyssey should not suffer again from factors outside his control. To what extent is this possible? [18 marks]

Examiner's hints
- In question 1, you need to consider the ways in which Odyssey could benefit from a new mission statement and the drawbacks as well. However, **focus on the company itself and consider its requirements.**
- For question 2, **try not to automatically agree or disagree with this question.** Examine both sides and consider, given Odyssey's situation, whether or not concern was warranted.
- In question 3, steer your response away from purely theoretical economic arguments. **A good evaluative response will consider the specific impacts to a company in Odyssey's markets.**
- Notice that question 4 directs you to consider the decision tree and '**any other relevant factors**'. This implies that a discussion involving the figures alone will be insufficient to gain full marks.
- **Question 5 is worth the most marks and requires you to make a mature consideration** of the ways in which it is possible for David Poole to control his situation, contrasted with factors that may prevent this from happening. A good evaluation will involve considering the business's requirements as well as David's.

Answers can be found on pages 100–104.

Answers to Questions to try

How to score full marks

1   (a)   Asset-led marketing occurs when a company identifies its major strengths and resources and then uses these to build its market position. For example, they will use market research but will only proceed to develop gaps and products that fit with areas where the business is already successful.

Market-led is different from this in that a company seeks to identify customer requirements and then develop products or services to meet those requirements. This means that they may end up diversifying or branching out into areas that are not their strengths as they attempt to satisfy customer needs.

In my opinion Sandra and Pablo are definitely market-led as everything they have done is in response to customer requirements. First, the initial start up came from responding to a friend's request, then they have expanded to meet the needs of the market and lastly they are again responding to a request from J D Wetherspoons. These are all market-led actions – they are not taking any initiative themselves, they only actually take action when the market asks them to.

> **Examiner's comment**
>
> This is a good response and justifies full marks for this question. The candidate has provided evidence that he has a good understanding of the terms by first offering brief definitions and then a further explanation of each. Paragraph three then contains a reasoned explanation for their choice. Notice as well that the candidate picks out relevant examples and information from the case study to justify his decision. This final piece of application secures full marks overall. It is possible to gain full marks using the same process but arguing that the company was asset-led, by using the example that the company is founded and developed on the strengths and resources of the people involved.

(b)   The marketing model requires that businesses employ a scientific and methodical approach to marketing – conducting market research, analysing data, setting strategies and tactics in light of company objectives – and then using a review process to determine if actions undertaken were successful.

This is quite a costly and time-consuming exercise that requires expertise and knowledge. Given Sandra's and Pablo's backgrounds, I doubt if they have the experience to undertake proper market research and analysis, let alone have the money to employ someone to do it for them. This isn't to say that it couldn't have helped them, just that I think it's unlikely they'd have ever been able to use it. They could have benefited as it might have helped them identify gaps and potential clients earlier, thus making an easy gradual expansion rather than this huge explosion to fill one order. It would also have enabled them to identify and concentrate on their most popular lines, so reducing costs such as wastage and boosting sales, particularly if they had adjusted recipes in light of customer feedback.

It would also have made Sandra and Pablo focus and plan for the future. Setting objectives and targets would provide more focus for the business. It would ensure that all those involved were working toward the same goal, again perhaps improving coordination but also motivation. People would know why they were there and what they were trying to achieve, so hopefully costs would fall and productivity rise. It would also help reduce the risk associated with what they were doing as they'd be able to use quantifiable techniques, like break-even analysis or cashflow forecasts, to help them make decisions and avoid mistakes. This would be of huge benefit as in extreme cases it could help them avoid potentially crippling events.

Overall, I feel that Pablo and Sandra might well benefit from setting objectives and devising plans and even conducting some market research, but they are only a small business still and so implementing the full marketing model might be beyond their pocket and expertise. This lack of expertise could cause them to make wrong decisions based on inaccurate research or analysis of data and so make mistakes that could be crucial to the survival of the business. So perhaps some benefit could be derived from a limited implementation of those parts that are most relevant to their current situation, such as producing a cashflow forecast.

2 (a)

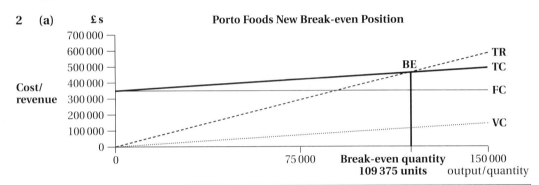

(b) From looking at the break-even chart, my first inclination would be to say, yes, the company should definitely accept the order. The break-even point is at 109,375 units and J D Wetherspoons £1.5 million pounds worth of products at a selling price of £4.00 each is a potential yearly order of 375 000 units. This means that Porto foods will make extra profits on every unit over break even or $(375\,000 - 109\,375) \times 3.20 =$ £850 000 total profit which is a huge improvement on the £25 000 they currently get, so this would imply they should definitely accept the order.

However, there seems to be a bit of a problem. Even if Porto foods invest in the new factory, buy or rent computer-aided machinery and employ specialised managers, their capacity will only be raised to 150 000 units, not the 375 000 that Wetherspoons require. This means that they wouldn't make such a large profit but actually only a maximum profit of £130 000, which is still very good. But, this assumes that Wetherspoons will be prepared to accept a delivery which is over 200 000 units short, which I doubt will happen.

In addition, this puts Porto foods in a very risky position because even if they supply Wetherspoons with 130 000 units, they cannot supply anyone else. Thus, if they lost the contract for any reason (like short deliveries), they would have no customers at all, but still have the expense of all the new expansion. The level of risk is also increased by the fact that Porto would have to get substantial bank loans to finance the project (£120 000). They already have loans of £12 000 and only have shareholder funds of £30 000. This would increase their gearing to 132 000/162 000 × 100 = 81.5% so they would be very highly geared.

I think that, as they can't meet the full contract anyway, there is a probability they might do all this and still not get the contract. Also, this rapid expansion and the massive interest payments on loans would put them at risk of overtrading and liquidity problems. For these reasons I don't think Porto foods should accept this order even though it looks very attractive on the surface. They should perhaps expand but not put all their eggs in one basket (customer). They need to expand more slowly and spread the risk.

> **Examiner's comment**
>
> This candidate's answer is highly focused throughout on the core issues of the question. From the opening sentence, the candidate has referred straight to the context of the question and begun an in-depth discussion of whether or not to accept the order.
>
> The following three paragraphs continue to raise relevant issues and analyse them with the provision of calculations to back up conclusions being made. In this type of question it is often necessary to provide numerical analysis as well as written analysis to achieve full marks for application.
>
> The candidate also realises that a definite judgment needs to be made. In this case it is not a single factor that has led to his decision but a consideration of the weight of argument against accepting the order.
>
> Note the candidate has not examined all the possible relevant arguments such as Pablo's questionable accounting ideas or calculated liquidity. However, this is not necessary, to gain full marks. Consideration of two or three points done well is sufficient to gain full marks.

3 **(a)** When assessing a workforce, there are several key areas to look at including: absenteeism, labour turnover and productivity. The problem here is that I'm only given productivity to look at so, although I can make some assessment, it may be unwise to reach an overall conclusion as I actually don't have all the evidence I'd like.

First of all, looking at Porto's key data, we can assess the number of customer complaints. These look promising, as they have fallen from 0.12% to 0.08%. This is actually better than it seems, as proportionally this is a 33% decrease in complaints from a basis where very few people actually complained anyway. People complain when there is something wrong with a product, such as it is broken or faulty. However, with food items people are more likely to complain about taste and quality. This fall shows that the employees are making better products as less people are complaining about taste or quality. From this I would assume that they must be getting better at their jobs and hence more effective.

This is backed up by the productivity figures themselves. We can see that the figure has risen from 11.8 to 15.5 over 6 months, which is good. But, if we look at this proportionally, the workers have actually managed to raise productivity in terms of portions made per hour by 31%. This is excellent and in terms of effectiveness means that the cost per product is less as there is less labour in each of them. Having lower costs means greater profits per product and thus I can conclude that the workforce is much more effective now than it was.

The wastage figure is also encouraging, though not as good as some of the other areas – it too has fallen by 5% from its original. This means the employees are making fewer mistakes and throwing less away. Therefore they must be taking greater care over what they are doing. This would imply that perhaps they are better trained or motivated and hence more effective.

I would say, therefore, that from the data given, the workforce appears to be much more effective in terms of productivity, complaints and waste. However, I don't know about absenteeism and labour turnover, but I would probably guess that a workforce doing so well in the other areas hasn't been leaving or taking time off.

(b) Computer-aided-manufacturing or CAM systems have several advantages and disadvantages to a firm like Porto.

First, CAM systems, although expensive to install, may in the long run prove more cost effective than personnel as they don't go off sick or take holidays, etc. – they can be used continuously and although they may break down, if brand new, this should be an infrequent occurrence as well as one that is fixed quickly. The case study also says it will raise productivity by 35% and capacity by 100%. This will cause the unit cost of each item to hopefully reduce, as shown by the break-even data in my earlier answer. Although the CAM machinery comes at a cost, the extra amount made offsets this to a lower unit cost overall, thus making each product more profitable.

The CAM equipment also seems to be designed to fulfil some of the more monotonous tasks like packaging the food. This might well release workers from boring, repetitive and de-motivating tasks. This, in turn, might make them feel happier and more motivated, doing more interesting work and so improve productivity even more.

However, as I discussed before, this equipment is very expensive and no doubt there are even further costs such as training the workforce to use it. This could cause Porto Foods short-term problems and loss of productivity as the equipment is installed and they learn how it works. At a time of hugely increased costs, having a stop or drop in production and thus in sales, and therefore cash and profits, is perhaps not the best thing.

The case study also mentions flexibility and this could be a problem as CAM systems are designed to carry out routine procedures. Therefore, if there is a sudden change in the market or in customers' needs and wants, (and Porto do seem to be market led) then they may be left with a lot of expensive machinery and costs to cover.

I do think that CAM is an appropriate strategy though for Porto Foods. They appear to have a happy and motivated staff and good relations, so introducing new technology should be easier than in some companies. Businesses need to grow and develop or else they may end up being left behind. At the moment Portuguese food may be a niche market but if it is successful, this won't be the case forever, so Porto need to expand to protect themselves in the long run. However, as I don't think they should accept the Wetherspoons order, I don't think they need to expand as fast and get as much CAM equipment immediately. I think they should take the option of renting some equipment, and giving the workforce time to get used to it whilst keeping initial costs down and minimising disruption. Then, as the equipment allows them to realise and fulfil more orders, they should introduce more and more, thus using a policy of gradual rather than sudden change.

4   First, looking at the people aspect of the business, there are several problems that they might encounter. One of the main problems here will be communications. At the moment its quite a small and friendly business with Sandra and Pablo taking a very much hands-on approach, but, as the case study says, as they grow they will have to take on specialist managers. This will add another layer to the hierarchy and so slow down communications. Also, much of the motivation gained from having a friendly family-type business may be lost as a more formal structure is put in place. From this, the business may well lose some of its flexibility and so affect its ability to respond to and meet customer requests, thus perhaps losing potential sales.

A second factor is that as they expand, they will need more employees – a big problem here is going to be finding employees. I imagine Portuguese food is quite a specialised thing and people are not going to be available to start work straight away. Porto are therefore going to have to spend money on recruiting and training each new factory employee, which is going to take time and money, raising costs and perhaps eating into any extra profit margins gained from increasing in size. I also think the company will experience problems if they grow too much as neither Sandra or Pablo are trained managers; Sandra is a cleaner and Pablo is a chef. Thus I think it unlikely that they have good knowledge of motivational technique and business organisation. This links to my earlier argument as to why I think there will be communication difficulties, as they are inexperienced, unless they are prepared to spent a great deal of money on training for themselves or perhaps hiring consultants.

My arguments so far also have an impact on the second part of this question – the effect on operational aspects. If the business experiences communication and coordination problems due to an expanded workforce and lack of experience, these are what are called diseconomies of scale. These cause inefficiency in the business's operations such as slow decision times or duplication of effort and misallocation of resources, all of which combine to force up unit costs and hence reduce profit margins.

Finally, moving to a new factory, installing new equipment and training new workers will all cause production to slow or stop completely, thus causing operational difficulties such as meeting customer orders or wasting perishable stock items. This could form a major cost to the company if the setting up of the new factory is not coordinated efficiently.

In conclusion then, I think Pablo's and Sandra's greatest problem is going to be their own lack of experience in coordinating and managing a bigger business. However, they do seem to have plus points like their willingness to take advice from their bank manager and hiring an accountant to help them in areas where they are not experts. So if they are able to obtain good advice and/or training for themselves they should hopefully succeed, as the evidence does suggest that their workers are motivated and that this must be a good company to work for.

3 The Report Question

How to score full marks

To: The Board of Directors, Cityspeed
From: Roberta Sparkes, Financial Advisor
Date: dd/mm/yy

A report examining the viability of the proposals to purchase new vehicles or a new depot

FINDINGS

Section 1 New vehicles

The first key data comes from Appendix A when it can be seen that Cityspeed's fleet is larger than Destina's and whilst Cityspeed have made more passenger journeys, Cityspeed's profits are falling, down 28.5% from 1998, whereas Destina's are rising. It also seems that despite a cheaper price, Cityspeed's number of passengers is falling whilst Destina's is going up. This would tend to suggest that passengers are willing to pay higher fares to travel on newer, better buses – Destina's buses being half the age of Cityspeed's and that the low-floor buses are worthwhile to attract customers as Destina currently has these in operation and Cityspeed does not.

A key point is that passengers seem willing to pay more to travel on newer buses, so if Cityspeed introduce new low-floor buses they may be able to raise prices and increase profits. Alongside this, new buses have a higher Average Rate of Return and Net Present Value than the depot option, again indicating that this option would be better for profits in the long run.

Similarly, we can consider the age of Cityspeed's buses as well and they are on **average** 10 years old. This, as highlighted, is an average so, for example, if we have one brand new bus we have another that is twenty years old. With seventy buses in total, Cityspeed must have some very old buses operating. Looking at Appendix B in conjunction with this, it seems that at least some of the problem of Cityspeed's declining profits is due to the age of their buses and the amount of breakdowns; in the year 2000 there were 364 breakdowns and a maintenance cost of approximately £8200 × 70 = £574 000 per year, which is more than the actual profits they made. With 15 new buses this figure will decline as brand new buses should be under warranty and should not break down anyway. Also we would not lose any customers and fare revenue to competitors from our buses breaking down. As a final bonus, there is forecasted to be a lot more old people in future years, so by investing in these new low-floor buses we stand a much greater chance of attracting them.

There are some drawbacks though. The 15 new buses will cost £1.5m and the business will have to borrow this money, as there are insufficient profits to finance the deal. This will push up the gearing ratio and cost the business in terms of interest payments. With declining profits as well, the company needs to ensure that the new buses will increase revenues more than they cost to finance. They also appear to cost more than the other option and so incur more of a risk. The other major drawback as compared to the depot is that the buses are a depreciating asset – after 15 years they will need replacing again, whereas a depot would not. Also, new buses do not solve the problem of the other buses breaking down, whereas the new depot has improved maintenance facilities.

Section 2 New depot

This too has several advantages. Not only does it come with improved maintenance facilities that should help lower costs, but it also does not need replacing in the way that buses do. Also, from Appendix D, it has a shorter payback period than new buses and so would start earning profits for the business much sooner. This is important when you consider the business's declining profits and return on capital employed.

A new depot and facilities, with more reliable buses, will help improve the company's image and so perhaps help prevent them losing more market share to Destina. Customers will be much more willing to use Cityspeed's service if they don't think buses will break down. Perhaps Cityspeed could even raise prices to match Destina's if they provide a better service. However, as the new depot just means that maintenance is better, not that the buses are newer, they are still going to need repairing and as they get even older they'll need repairing more frequently.

Cityspeed have been offered £2m pounds for their old depot by a developer. However, the new depot would be two miles outside the city centre and I think a city centre location is a major benefit to a bus company as this is where most people want to travel from and to.

Section 3 Recommendations

From the evidence, I would say that Cityspeed's major problem is the age of its buses and that getting a new depot does nothing to solve this. With new buses we can compete head to head with Destina and replace some of our old fleet. This cuts down on maintenance costs, keeps customers happy with better transport and fewer breakdowns as well as perhaps charging a higher price or being more competitive by still charging a lower one and gaining back market share.

However, I would like to recommend that Cityspeed do not buy 15 low-floor buses but, say, buy 20 new ordinary ones. Being ordinary they will be cheaper to purchase so we can replace more of their older buses, cutting even more costs. People won't refuse to get on them because they are not low-floor – if they are waiting for a bus and one of Cityspeed's arrives, they will get on it, low floor or not. Thus, with better buses and a better service, Cityspeed's reputation and profits should increase.

Finally, Cityspeed is a bigger company than Destina so if all else fails, Cityspeed could launch a takeover and control all the buses and market in Traverton. This is not my first recommendation as I think it might be very expensive, but it is something to consider at your next Board meeting.

R. Sparkes, Financial Advisor.

Examiner's comment

This is an excellent example of how to structure a report and provide a full-mark response. The candidate's report format is fine and the approach to the question is well thought through, logical and easy to follow. Alongside this, she interrelates information from the different appendices as she considers each option in turn and arrives at a logical conclusion. The examiner is able to follow the candidate's thought processes throughout and thus she gains high marks for evaluation.

Notice that the candidate has not tried to include every piece of information from the appendices; she has picked out only those items she feels are most relevant to the investigation being conducted. Nor have figures been copied out, except for a calculation. The candidate has considered the information and related her discussion directly to how it impacts on the decision to be made.

The final evaluation is a suitable conclusion to the report even though it is not one of the choices offered. This candidate has considered the business's situation and provided a mature, well thought out and compelling rationale for why she is making her particular recommendations.

🎯 How to score full marks

1   The first and most obvious benefit of the Internet is the contribution it can make to the selling activities of the organisation. The Internet allows a business to reach a global network of customers and advertise their products in a very cost effective manner; it enables many businesses that would traditionally pass goods down the supply chain to direct sell to customers and thus obtain a greater number of customers and market share. There are some costs involved, such as setting up a web page and purchasing security equipment to enable encrypted transactions to take place, but these are minimal compared to the vast number of potential customers.

However, this does not mean that the company is actually going to gain all these customers as it is likely that their competitors are also doing the same, so perhaps it is just a different way of reaching the same people. In this case there is a definite advantage if you have this capability and others do not, but probably very little advantage, just extra costs, if everybody has it.

Another advantage that the Internet does give businesses though, is access to information and data, and the speed at which it can be obtained, This can give a business a competitive advantage over rivals; if they have access to information their rivals do not, perhaps they could identify a trend sooner and so be able to cater to consumers' needs quicker, thus temporarily cornering the market and boosting their sales and profits.

Another big advantage, and a common use of the Internet, is to advertise for new employees. This certainly allows the business to reach a much wider range of potential employees at a fraction of the cost of advertising in national newspapers. However, you are perhaps only targeting a specific group of IT conversant people; the actual employee you really want may well only look in newspapers.

Not everything about the Internet is brilliant though. Employees and managers can suffer from information and communication overload, which makes decision making even slower than previously or breaks established communication pathways – if not all managers have access to e-mail, some may be excluded from communications and then start to make incorrect decisions and become de-motivated in their work. Similarly, there has been a lot of controversy in the press about employees wasting time at work in a non-productive activity such as surfing the 'net' and e-mailing friends. This is a cost to the business in lost productive time and wages.

Whether or not the Internet is beneficial to business is, I think, dependent on whether it provides the business with a competitive advantage, whether it is used in conjunction with, not as a replacement for, traditional methods, and on the way in which it is managed in the workplace. The Internet is a tool like any other and if used and employed effectively should bring benefits but, if misused and abused, it will probably be detrimental to the smooth operations of the organisation. Overall, the Internet can help a business save costs and gain information and employees and it can help contact customers but it cannot give customers any more money to spend, so its benefits are limited. Of course it is of no benefit if a business does not have the money to install it and many small businesses do not. The Internet thus puts them at a competitive disadvantage to rivals who do.

Examiner's comment

This is an example of how to write a successful essay. The main body of the essay is taken with analysing and considering the way in which the Internet could benefit business, but note how in these first three or four paragraphs the candidate contrasts each benefit with a short consideration of limitations or includes some judgment regarding the level of benefit to be obtained. Thus this candidate is providing analysis and evaluation as he proceeds through the question.

The final paragraphs consider the drawbacks the Internet revolution has brought to organisations and thus provides a nicely balanced approach to the question with the last evaluative paragraph as a summary of the main points and the introduction of an awareness of wider issues such as the effect on many smaller companies.

---

4 To many, this would seem a silly question. 'Of course this isn't desirable', they would say. By transferring manufacturing overseas, UK workers are going to lose their jobs, causing unemployment in the UK and an economic downturn or recession. This would occur as unemployed people have less money to spend so demand falls, so companies cut back and make even more people unemployed. Couple this with the downward multiplier effect and the level of demand in the economy, and hence jobs and prosperity also decline.

This would also have negative impacts like the government raising taxes, for example, as they have more unemployed people to support – again reducing companies' own profits or also reducing customers' disposable income so having a further effect on profits. There may also be social impacts like declining health or rising crime as people suffer from declining standards of living.

But what about the business itself? They are moving abroad probably because they can get cheaper labour or would be nearer to raw materials so they can get them more quickly and easily. All this means cheaper costs. The business may have been attracted by foreign governments with grants, subsidies, cheap loans or preferential tax rates. Add all these together and what do you get – *more profits*. This is good for the company as they can retain more for investment, perhaps develop new products, diversifying and spreading their risk or even paying more money to shareholders. This is great if you are a shareholder, as you personally become richer.

What about the people in the foreign country as well? They will love it; they've now got jobs and a growing economy with a better standard of living. The foreign government gets more in income tax and so perhaps they can raise health or education standards in their country.

So what about us, the customer? Well this could go either way. Perhaps the company is going to be nice to us and pass some of these cost savings on in the form of cheaper prices, which is great because then we can buy even more. Perhaps the company's increased investment means we get more choice, or newer improved products for the same price (or cheaper). However, what about the quality? Surely cheaper workers will make lower quality goods and then the customer will suffer. Well, maybe, but it isn't necessarily true that just because they're cheaper to employ they are bad at their work. Probably they just have a lower standard of living in their economy so they don't need (or expect) as high a wage level. With training and equipment why shouldn't they be just as good at their job?

Perhaps, and this is a key point, the only way the business could survive in its really competitive market was if it did move to a cheaper location. Surely this is better than no business at all. Similarly perhaps the business has not gone anywhere cheaper, but instead to somewhere where workers are better qualified and trained. In this case we might get better products.

The answer to the question of whether this is desirable or not then is that it depends totally on who and where you are – a shareholder or employee, a worker in this country or in the country the business is going to.

Examiner's comment

I would not advocate copying this candidate's style of writing, but, despite this, he does get his points across and they are very well made. The candidate focuses on the core of the question throughout his answer in his consideration of who benefits and who doesn't. This is coupled with the fact that the candidate doesn't make automatic assumptions about why this is taking place. He examines different stakeholder groups and considers the impact and effect on that group, which is then compared and contrasted with the effect on an opposing group.

Despite the style of writing, the structure is good with clearly defined arguments broken into paragraphs. The evaluative statement at the end is not very long, but really it doesn't need to be. The candidate has hit the nail right on the head.

How to score full marks

1   A mission statement is a document, which lays out the long-term goals that the business wishes to achieve. It provides the focus around which all strategic plans and objectives are set. This helps the business to communicate to employees in what direction the business is trying to develop and as such helps provide a common sense of purpose, so that all areas of the business are working toward the same goal. This makes for a more efficient allocation and use of resources as it allows managers and employees to direct their efforts toward the business's aims. In particular, managers can now make decisions with a clear understanding of what the desired end result should be. The decisions taken should be much more accurate and perhaps made more quickly, as alternatives that don't fit the mission can be discarded. So, the decision making should be more cost effective and less time consuming.

Also, mission statements can be used as a basis for motivating workers. Employees who understand why they are there, what they are doing and what is their role in the organisation are much more motivated than employees who lack direction and focus. This can therefore bring productive benefits to the organisation and increased efficiency, reducing costs and perhaps generating ideas for increased productive gains, as the workers are happy in what they are doing. Similarly, the setting of objectives allows performance management and the identification of strengths and weaknesses to take place, as well as developing a reward system to motivate workers even further.

However, it is no good just writing a mission statement, this just takes time and money for no reward, the statement then has to be communicated and used – if employees are not aware of it then it does not provide a sense of direction. In Odyssey's case it appears to *'hang on the boardroom wall'* and there is no mention of it actually being used at all. Alongside this, it is irrelevant to large areas of the business, as it makes no mention of the hotels, so in this respect it is actually no longer appropriate.

In conclusion, I think Odyssey would benefit from re-writing their mission statement, as it needs updating, though perhaps not if they sell off the hotels, but it then actually needs to be used and communicated regularly. This is because in the pub trade, staff changes frequently, particularly at the lower levels. To be of any use as a focus, new staff and all managers need to be aware of the mission statement. The firm will only benefit from using a mission statement if it is realistic and then used. Otherwise it will just cost time and money to produce.

> **Examiner's comment**
>
> This is a good, clear and to the point response. The candidate shows a good understanding of the meaning of the term and the benefits and drawbacks that can and do occur. However, this is by no means a comprehensive answer – there are several points that the candidate doesn't fully investigate, such as the use of mission statements as PR exercises. This doesn't prevent her attaining full marks as the candidate has developed several points and considered the implications.
>
> The candidate has again used specific examples from the case study to strengthen her findings and conclusion. This is not the same as just copying or re-wording the case study text; in this example it is used as part of the argument.
>
> The candidate has identified that this question requires an evaluative response and has provided an excellent judgement directly relevant to the context of the type of business given.

2   Every business organisation has responsibilities to different stakeholder groups, one of these being the shareholders, who are the owners and key investors in the business. Shareholders are primarily interested in profits and seeing a return on their investment by increase in the value of shares. It appears that Frances' actions could therefore have had several impacts that would have affected the directors.

By being more socially responsible, such as considering the effect of business operations on the local community or the effect of decisions on employees, Frances could actually have increased the costs incurred by the business – for example, not making workers redundant, or letting workers go during the off-peak season, by perhaps paying retaining fees or placing them on reduced hours. Alongside this, there may be increased costs in terms of the community, such as keeping the environment clean, and tidying up after tourists. These increased costs would have served to reduce profits for the business and so perhaps have conflicted with the shareholders aims.

However, the case study does highlight the free publicity and TV coverage that Frances got, **several times**. This free advertising on TV would in itself be worth thousands, if not hundreds of thousands, of pounds and help the business generate many more sales at no expense to themselves. It also states that the hotels raised the profile of the whole firm, so Odyssey's pubs would have benefited from this increased publicity and hence extra sales as well. This would have had two effects. Perhaps it would have generated enough extra profits to offset some of the costs of being more socially responsible, but also by making the chain more high profile and successful, the value of shares on the market will have risen as well, thus benefiting shareholders two-fold.

As a final point, employees find working for a socially responsible business more motivating as they feel more secure in their jobs and more of their needs are catered for. This again would benefit shareholders in terms of increased productivity, less waste and mistakes, a better quality service to customers (very important in the hotel industry) and a more loyal workforce so less labour turnover, all or which would help improve and maintain profits.

The difficulty comes in that a business needs to adopt and carry through a responsible stance for a period of time before the benefits start to be generated. This means that in the short term there is a cost to the business, and perhaps a drop in profits, before any benefits are seen. This could give the directors cause for concern, especially as it is very likely that they are shareholders as well.

Perhaps then, the directors were correct to be concerned if this initial drop in profits had occurred and Frances had not communicated the long-term possible benefits to be gained. But as the hotels appeared to be successful, and it was only 'one or two' who were concerned, then I do not suppose they were right to be concerned as the business appears to have been a successful venture until the rises in inflation, interest and exchange rates and all these are factors outside Frances' control.

> **Examiner's comment**
>
> When it comes to questions regarding topic areas like social responsibilities and business ethics, candidates often find it impossible to keep their own opinions and ideologies to themselves. They will often attack the question and therefore find it difficult to respond in a constructive and rational manner.
>
> This candidate, though, has considered the argument in a non-personal and logical way. Analysis comes from the consideration of opposite views and discussion of their impact and implications for Odyssey. Good evaluation is made stemming from the consideration of short- and long-term effects, the position of the business and the position of the directors as well. Again this helps to put the candidate's response in context.
>
> Finally, the obvious structure of separate paragraphs for separate points helps the examiner follow the development through the entire question.

3   The impact that this is going to have on Odyssey is entirely dependent on what action the government and other bodies take to combat inflation.

First and most likely, is the fact that the Bank of England may raise interest rates. This is going to have several effects. On the pub scene, if customers have less disposable income from increased interest payments on loans and mortgages then they are going to cut back spending on luxuries such as going out, and stay at home and watch a video instead. This will cut back Odyssey's revenue from pub sales. However, they may also gain custom as some customers switch from higher luxuries like restaurant meals to pub meals instead. The case study indicates that Odyssey's main customer base is 'new, younger customers'. This market segment is less likely to have mortgages, etc. and also less likely to cut down on going out, so in reality the effect here could be very little indeed. In fact, Odyssey may actually gain as their hotels are at the 'no frills' end of the market; customers will switch from more expensive hotels to more basic accommodation, thus increasing customer numbers and hence profits.

The difficulty would come if the rise in interest rates, caused a corresponding rise in exchange rates, so making the pound more expensive for foreigners. This would deter foreigners from taking UK-based holidays and as Odyssey's hotels are focused on attracting customers from Western Europe then this could have a decline in their demand and consequently a serious fall in sales revenue. This is unlikely to be replaced by British customers as they, too, are facing declining disposable income and so would not be spending money on luxury items like holidays in hotels – they will drop to the bottom end of the holiday market like caravans or self catering or perhaps go abroad where their pound is stronger. Thus the hotels are going to suffer all round.

However, interest rates don't have to change – these, after all, are controlled by the Bank of England. The government could take its own measures to affect the level of aggregate demand in the economy by raising taxes or cutting back on expenditure. This also will affect the amount of disposable income of consumers and cause a downward multiplier effect. Again the effect is much more likely to be on the more income elastic product which is holidays, not pubs. So again it is likely that Odyssey's would lose sales and corresponding profits. The benefit would be that exchange rates could stay stable and so the demand for hotel holidays from abroad would also remain the same.

The exact effect on Odyssey's then depends very much on what action is actually taken and what aspect of the business's operation you are considering; pub and hotels have different income elasticities and so will behave differently from each other. This is one of the advantages of having a diversified portfolio in that it offers some protection from economic downturns and changes. Furthermore, this is also highly dependent on what the EU is doing. If most of the hotel customers come from within the EU then the performance of the Euro economy and their interest rates and level of inflation will have a massive impact on foreigners taking holidays abroad and as there is no information in the text about this I am unable to judge what the impact may be.

Examiner's comment

Again this answer does not consider all the possible points such as an effect on investments and the cost to the company of borrowed monies, where the impact is dependent on how highly geared the company is. However, the response does examine three relevant points in a great depth; the candidate shows a very good tactic of considering the different products and markets as separate items, rather than a company as a whole. This then leads to making the final judgments at the end, which show a good awareness of market operations and the wider issues that influence their operation.

The key aspect of this response is how the candidate has avoided just a purely theoretical answer but actually tailored their response exactly to Odyssey and their circumstances. Similarly, they have answered the correct question. It is very easy to respond to this as what would the impact of inflation be, but this is not what is actually being asked for and responses along these lines would gain little reward.

The evaluation that the candidate cannot arrive at a definite conclusion is a valid one in this case, as the candidate has raised and explained a legitimate reason why, it is not just a throw-away statement.

---

4   From the decision tree it can be seen that from the various options given, that doing nothing and marketing to the United States are not viable courses of action as they both result in a net loss overall. This means that the decision comes down to whether or not to keep the hotel chain at an expected return of £350 000 pounds profit per year or to sell the chain for an immediate payment of £5 million pounds from Clarke's.

This is a difficult decision to make. First, the £5 million pounds would no doubt provide a much needed boost to Odyssey's profits and cash flow. However, this is what is known as low quality or one-off profit, that is, it cannot be repeated. The danger is that they will get extra profits this year, but what are they going to do in future to replace it? The extra money could be used to expand the pub chain I suppose, but the case study does not say how many pubs the company already has and I know (as my Dad is a landlord) that breweries are limited to the amount of pubs they can now own, so perhaps investing here isn't an option. Even if they can expand, it then puts Odyssey in danger of placing all their eggs in one basket – they will lose the benefits of spreading the risk through a diversified portfolio.

Alternatively, they could use the £5 million to diversify elsewhere, but this then increases the risk, as they will be entering a market in which they have no experience, Ansoff's matrix outlines this as being the most risky course of action to take, so perhaps they'd be better off not risking £5 million in this way.

Keeping the hotels means that they would be receiving £350 000 pounds estimated profit per year; admittedly on this basis it would take 14 years to raise the £5 million that would be foregone. However, this would be high quality repeatable profits year on year and could improve even more – if exchange rates improve, to £1 million per year, which although, maybe not immediately, is bound to happen eventually. Secondly, the company gets to keep a £5 million pound asset that increases their balance sheet strength. Hopefully the value of property will increase over time as well. This will enable them to meet shareholder aims of paying dividends and increasing worth.

Also, by keeping the chain of hotels it enables the company to maintain its promise of behaving in a socially responsible manner. To go back on this promise or to sell the chain could result in a lot of adverse publicity, just as they gained in the beginning, which would have a knock-on effect to their pub sales. Also, it may adversely affect the motivation levels of employees who remain, as they would become concerned about their own job security. Keeping the hotels allows the company to fulfil the needs of other stakeholder groups as well as shareholders.

The case study says that the hotels currently break even; they are forecasted to make a profit, which could get even better, and allow the company to hold on to a valuable asset whilst meeting the needs of many stakeholders. Selling the hotels enables a one-off gain of £5 million but I don't know what the company would do with it. I would recommend that the company keep the hotels, use some of the profits and hire a new managing director who knows the market and how to handle a diverse organisation. This is because David was already 50 in 1995 and he probably will want to retire again soon, so perhaps he shouldn't make the main decisions regarding the businesses future for the next decade or so.

Examiner's comment

This response provides a good example of how information not learned in class can provide a useful basis for discussion and development. Lessons learned from outside experiences such as work placements, jobs or Young Enterprise activities could be used as relevant material in these questions.

The candidate has considered each option looking at the positives and negatives and analysed the outcome each may have on Odyssey's position. Again the candidate has identified that the question requires consideration of 'other factors' to gain full marks and so has done this by considering the stakeholder positions developed in an earlier response.

The evaluation is a sound decision that stems from the candidate's own line of reasoning and is a sensible option to put forward. The idea of hiring a new MD is put forward rationally and the candidate has provided detailed the reasons why.

A point to note, though, is that it would be perfectly acceptable to argue the alternative view, that Odyssey should sell the chain given the difficult economic situation and the benefits a £5 million injection could bring to the pub side of operations. Similarly, a viable argument would be the consideration of benefits to be gained from selling off peripherals and concentrating on core activities.

5   I think given the market areas that Odyssey's operate in this is going to be a very difficult objective to attain.

In question 3 I have already considered how a business like Odyssey's could be affected by external factors such as interest rates and exchange rates. Obviously the determination of these factors is outside David's control as these are external influences over the business and the environment in which it operates. However, it is possible that David could make sure that Odyssey did not suffer, or was prepared for, such fluctuations by carrying out contingency planning so that when a crisis or economic downturn occurs, the business is already prepared for it and knows how to react. Thus, the business can respond quickly and efficiently, maybe not escaping harm completely, but by being pro-active rather than reactive they can put in place strategies that would act to minimise the effect of changing external influences.

However, effective contingency planning relies heavily upon having accurate information and forecasts so that plans can be developed, as well as the right type of management to implement those plans when necessary. This involves a considerable cost and commitment of resources by the company and it is an ongoing cost as well. Plans need to developed, reviewed and adjusted in light of events that occur and new information that is obtained. This requires backing from shareholders and the rest of the board as funds used to make contingency plans cannot be used elsewhere. Similarly, I think David has to be realistic; the list of factors that could occur that are outside David's control is virtually endless. He needs to be sensible and perhaps only plan for those events that are likely, such as recession or perhaps a bomb scare in a pub. If he spent all his time planning for possible events such as a petrol strike, the BSE crises, foot and mouth, etc. he would have no time left for running the business.

Businesses like Odyssey are affected not only by economic influences but, as they deal directly with the public, they are affected by social and demographic changes as well. Again, through good research and planning many of these can be dealt with, but who knows what the next trend or fashion in drinks is going to be. I also don't think Odyssey have the spare resources to be able to research and forecast every possibility.

I think that the only way David can ensure that the business never suffers from factors outside his control is to shut the company, otherwise something is always going to occur somewhere that you haven't thought of. David can minimise the impact of these events by obtaining accurate data, making contingency plans and having a well trained and effective management team.

Examiner's comment

The introductory sentence contains no content, but perhaps serves as a useful launch pad to get the candidate into the question. In this response it appears at first that the candidate has provided a fairly one-sided response; their opening statement influences this. However, on consideration, they have provided lines of argument concerning how David might achieve his objective contrasted with why they think it may be difficult.

Again the candidate is providing a good analysis of the question in context by considering the type of market and products, as well as the resources available to the company.

The final paragraph sums up the important factors and places them in context by making an extreme comparison. The key factor here though is that candidate has not just argued 'yes he can' or 'no he can't' but has tried to provide a thoughtful conclusion.